DATE DUE

Exploring Phenomenology

SECOND EDITION

DAVID STEWART

ALGIS MICKUNAS

Exploring
Phenomenology

SECOND EDITION

A GUIDE TO

THE FIELD AND ITS

LITERATURE

OHIO UNIVERSITY PRESS

ATHENS

Ohio University Press books are printed on acid-free paper. ⊗

Library of Congress Cataloging-in-Publication Data

Stewart, David, 1938–
Exploring phenomenology : a guide to the field and its literature
David Stewart, Algis Mickunas. —2nd ed.
p.   cm.
Includes bibliographical references.
ISBN 0-8214-0961-1. —ISBN 0-8214-0962-X (pbk.)
1. Phenomenology.   2. Bibliography—Best books—Phenomenology.
3. Philosophy, Modern—20th century.   4. Bibliography—Best Books—
Philosophy, Modern—20th century.   5. Phenomenology—Bibliography.
6. Philosophy, Modern—20th century—Bibliography.   I. Mickunas,
Algis.   II. Title.

B829.S67   1990   89-49294
142'.7—dc20   CIP

Printed in the United States of America

CONTENTS

PREFACE

This book is written for the nonspecialist and for the generally educated reader who wants to know more about phenomenology, the kind of philosophy that considers anything appearing to consciousness as a legitimate field of inquiry. Phenomenology may not yet be a household word in this country, but with its offspring, existentialism, phenomenology offers one of the two major alternatives in contemporary philosophy. The other, variously called logical analysis or linguistic analysis (although adherents to that point of view might not be comfortable at being subsumed under such broad categories), focuses on the problems of philosophy as having been engendered by lack of clarity in the proper use of language. Linguistic analysis sees the solution to philosophical problems as lying in the clarification of language and the resolution of the ambiguity inherent in the way traditional philosophic problems have been posed. Such broad generalizations of a multifaced point of view are open to the charge of oversimplification; a better introduction to the origins and methods of analytic philosophy will be provided by the companion volume in this series, *The Analytic Tradition in Philosophy,* by Michael Corrado.

EXPLORING PHENOMENOLOGY, although oriented toward the person for whom phenomenology is a new area of inquiry, is not offered as a substitute for reading the works of major phenomenologists themselves. Nothing can take the place of that. The intention of this effort is to serve as a guide to the student and, if it is successful, to provide a beginning point on which he can build.

One of the difficulties encountered in a first reading of phenomenology is the bewildering variety of technical terms present in the literature. As is true of any specialized discipline, phenomenology has developed its own philosophical jargon. This was not due to mere pedantry but resulted from the need to distinguish phenomenological insights from prevailing philosophical views which were so wedded to traditional terminology. Every attempt has been made in this book to suppress this highly specialized vocabulary and to define it in detail whenever such terms are introduced. There is risk in this attempt, for technical terms are a kind of shorthand for the expression of complex ideas. Encouragement in this effort, however, is offered by C. E. M. Joad in his book *The Recovery of Belief,* in which he remarked that "any philosopher who takes the trouble to master the art of writing clearly and is at pains to exercise it, can explain most of the things in philosophy to any reader of intelligence and goodwill, provided that the philosopher understands what he is writing about." Whether we have been successful in following Joad's advice is left for the reader to judge.

A major part of this book is devoted to the literature in the field of phenomenology, and the lengthy bibliographies at the end of each chapter are intended to provide a guide to all the major areas of phenomenological research. No claim is made, however, for the exhaustiveness of these bibliographies. Even though phenomenology is a rather recent philosophical movement, the literature produced by the movement is massive, particularly in Europe where it first gained widespread attention. In compiling the bibliographic sections of this book, selectivity rather than comprehensiveness was our goal. Major emphasis is placed on works in English, and if a book is available in English translation, no mention is made of its original foreign-language edition, except in the case of volumes in the Husserliana and Phaenomenologica series, which constitute major publication efforts in the field. Where existing bibliographies are available in particular areas relevant to phenomenology, they have been cited with no attempt to duplicate their entries. In determining which of the foreign-language materials should be included, we have selected those works which have had the greatest impact on the development of phenomenology and are most widely cited by philosophers working within the phenomenological tradition. Journal articles are included whenever they add a significant insight to an understanding of phenomenology. All bibliographical entries are numbered to facilitate cross references. The entries are annotated except those titles that clearly indicate the contents of the work and some foreign-language works, whose titles tend to be more descriptive than those of works published in English. No annotation is offered for the works cited in the Appendix inasmuch as it is mainly a guide to further reading, whereas the works most directly relevant to the development of phenomenology are included in the bibliographies following each chapter. The guiding principle throughout has been to provide a manageable as well as useful guide to the literature most accessible and most helpful to the student of phenomenology in this country.

Whatever value this work has was aided to a considerable degree by Carolyn Dyer's careful typing of the manuscript and by Kay Horr's scrupulous preparation of the index, services for which the authors wish to express their appreciation.

CHAPTER 1
GENERAL
THEMES
OF
PHENOMENOLOGY

Anyone about to venture forth on a new journey would be well advised to get a general idea of where he is going, to grasp the lay of the land, and to familiarize himself with some of the principal landmarks. As good a place to begin as any is the meaning of the term *phenomenology* itself. It is derived from two Greek words: *phainomenon* (an "appearance") and *logos* ("reason" or "word," hence a "reasoned inquiry"). Phenomenology is indeed a reasoned inquiry which discovers the inherent essences of appearances. But what is an *appearance?* The answer to this question leads to one of the major themes of phenomenology: an appearance is anything of which one is conscious. Anything at all which appears to consciousness is a legitimate area of philosophical investigation. Moreover, an appearance is a manifestation of the essence of that of which it is the appearance. Surprising as it may sound, other philosophic points of view have refused to make this move.

This is not to imply that previous philosophies had ignored the problem of consciousness; far from it. The philosophers of the seventeenth and eighteenth centuries were extremely concerned with this question, but

—according to phenomenologists—they made a fatal error in method when they treated consciousness as merely a substance among other substances in the natural world. Descartes, as is well known, divided all of reality into two substances—thinking substance (mind, or consciousness) and extended substance (bodies), and this division set the stage for the problems in modern philosophy which center around the question of how these two substances can have an epistemological relationship. One implication of this Cartesian dualism was a shift in emphasis away from conscious experience to objective realities as they are in themselves, with the result that consciousness was virtually ignored as a significant area of investigation in its own right. By the nineteenth century, the "subjective" factor in experience was ignored as irrelevant and of no philosophic importance.

As a result a kind of philosophy developed which attempted to treat consciousness as an empirical phenomenon that can be investigated by the quantitative methods of natural science. Phenomenology rejects this approach and insists that the quantitative methods of science are not adequate to treat the nature of consciousness—principally for two reasons: (1) consciousness itself is not an object among other objects in nature, and (2) there are conscious phenomena which cannot be dealt with adequately by means of the quantitative methods of experimental science. The exclusive application of the scientific method as adequate to an investigation of all reality excludes those phenomena which are not open to this kind of analysis. In short, phenomenology does not limit its investigations only to those realities which are objective in a materialistic or naturalistic sense. Consequently, phenomenology offers a considerable broadening of the range of philosophical inquiry inasmuch as phenomenologists make no assumptions about what is or is not real; they rather begin with the content of consciousness—whatever that content may be —as valid data for investigation.

Phenomenology, however, is not a rigid school or uniform philosophic discipline. There is great diversity in the points of view of thinkers who could be classified under the general rubric *phenomenology,* and the most proper description of this way of approaching philosophy is the phenomenological "movement"—as indeed the term is used by the noted phenomenologist Herbert Spiegelberg in his historical introduction to phenomenology.[1] The diversity of points of view held by philosophers working within the phenomenological tradition makes a summary of major phenomenological tenets difficult, and one should be aware that other descriptions of phenomenology which focus on different areas of

1. Spiegelberg, *The Phenomenological Movement: A Historical Introduction.* *See* n̟o. 101.

common emphasis might also be given. It is not even the case that all phenomenologists would agree that the themes mentioned here are the most important ones. But this state of affairs attests to the dynamic diversity of ways the phenomenological approach to philosophy has been applied. With these caveats in mind, one can characterize phenomenological philosophy as centering on the following basic themes: a return to the traditional tasks of philosophy, the search for a philosophy without presuppositions, the intentionality of consciousness, and the refusal of the subject-object dichotomy.

A RETURN TO THE TRADITIONAL TASKS OF PHILOSOPHY

Those who come to a study of phenomenology expecting to find a strange and bizarre kind of philosophy may be shocked to discover that phenomenologists are doing nothing other than what philosophy—at its best—has always done. This is most certainly what Edmund Husserl, a major figure in the origins of phenomenology, meant when he made the following observation in his article on phenomenology for the *Encyclopaedia Britannica:* "Phenomenological philosophy is but developing the mainsprings of old Greek philosophy, and the supreme motive of Descartes. These have not died."[2] One of the mainsprings of Greek philosophy was the conviction that philosophy is a search for wisdom, or true knowledge, and the belief that philosophy's task is to attempt to understand the nature of the cosmos and man's position in it. "Philosophy begins in wonder," Plato observed, meaning that it is philosophy's task to articulate the questions arising out of the depths of the human spirit itself. Man desires knowledge of himself and his world, and it is philosophy's task to achieve such understanding.

By the end of the nineteenth century, however, the scope of philosophy had become severely limited. The spectacular success of natural science in describing the physical world had given rise to the conviction that there was nothing about the world that was not capable of being investigated by empirical means. Philosophy, according to a widely accepted position, should therefore confine itself to empirical statements, a view phenomenologists referred to as "scientism." Philosophy was no longer seen as an independent discipline with a task of its own. Whereas some medieval thinkers saw philosophy as the handmaiden of theology, many modern thinkers—especially by the end of the nineteenth and beginning of the twentieth century—saw philosophy as the handmaiden of science. Philos-

2. Husserl, "Phenomenology." *See* no. 37.

ophy's role, in this view, was not to question the assumptions of science or to clarify the concepts implicit in scientific activity but only to explicate certain problems arising in logic. But this emphasis on logic as the only proper tool for philosophic inquiry led to a distortion of the role of logic. If a problem cannot be formulated in logical terms, then it is at best only a pseudoproblem and at worst a meaningless collection of words. Whereas this point of view did not reach its zenith until the first part of the twentieth century when the logical positivists formulated their verifiability principle,[3] the roots of this attitude reach well back into the nineteenth century. In its most extreme formulations, logical positivism maintained that the only statements that are meaningful are those expressing propositions verifiable either (1) by an appeal to the senses (i.e., verifiable empirically) or (2) by definition (i.e., analytically true). All other statements, according to positivists, are meaningless. Traditional philosophic efforts directed to ethical, metaphysical, and religious inquiries were relegated to the trash bin.

The positivists' approach represents a considerable narrowing of philosophic activity. To be sure, philosophy itself had been guilty of excesses, especially in the early part of the nineteenth century when the German idealists—most notably Hegel—constructed elaborate and comprehensive systems of thought which claimed not only totality but absoluteness as well. In his *Phenomenology of Mind,* Hegel used the term *phenomenology* to describe the coming to absolute self-awareness of mind or spirit. This sense of the word phenomenology is most decidedly not the meaning it had when used by Husserl and his successors. Failure to recognize the vast difference in the meaning of phenomenology as used by Hegel and its meaning for Husserl and his followers will only lead to confusion.

A PHILOSOPHY
WITHOUT
PRESUPPOSITIONS

Every rational activity begins with assumptions about the nature of its activity, the object being investigated, and the method appropriate to this kind of inquiry. Physical science, for example, presumes the existence of physical objects to be investigated by empirical means. Idealistic philosophy, by presuming a distinction between appearance and reality, is led to conclude that only appearances are known, and since the content

3. *See* A. J. Ayer, *Language, Truth, and Logic,* 2d ed. (New York: Dover, n.d.). See especially ch. 5, pp. 87–103.

of such knowledge is ideas, one can account for reality perfectly well only in terms of minds and ideas. The temptation of science—especially in view of the spectacular success of its method—is to extend its presuppositions to everything. In its extreme form this amounts to the assertion that *all* reality is capable of being investigated by empirical means. Minds are merely complex machines; thought itself is in principle explainable as the function of certain biophysical processes. The devastating implications this view has for an understanding of the nature of logical thought itself were one of the problems with which Husserl was concerned in the early years of his work. Philosophical idealism, on the other hand, faces a similar temptation but with opposite conclusions. With its emphasis on minds and ideas, it is tempted to interpret all reality in such terms.

In both cases, presuppositions inherent in the method of approach itself lead to certain assumptions about the nature of reality. These assumptions must be challenged, and it should be philosophy's task to question all such presuppositions—even its own. This recognition of philosophy's role in challenging the basic assumptions of all rational endeavors was one of the motivating principles in Edmund Husserl's development of phenomenology. Husserl's insight was that for philosophy to be equal to this task, it must free itself from all such presuppositions.

There are many kinds of presuppositions, and there is even a sense in which absolute freedom from presuppositions is impossible, for the view that a philosophy without presuppositions is possible is itself a kind of presupposition. What Husserl and subsequent phenomenologists were rejecting were those presuppositions concerning the nature of the real. Phenomenology's approach is to suspend all judgments about such matters until they can be founded on a more certain basis. This suspension of the "natural attitude," as Husserl called it, was labeled by him the phenomenological "epoche" (from the Greek word used by Stoic philosophy to refer to abstention of belief). Having made this epoche, philosophy begins its description and clarification of consciousness unencumbered by the assumptions of the natural attitude. (A more detailed discussion of the epoche is found in the next chapter.) The radical nature of this approach to philosophy is well summarized by the noted phenomenologist Marvin Farber when he points out that the phenomenological epoche gives philosophy a starting point free from the presuppositions which mask hidden assumptions about the nature of reality.

> What is assumed at this point? Not the spatio-temporal world; none of the scientific theories which are used to interpret the world of existence; no independent or continuous existence; no other human beings; not one's own bodily existence or empirically conditioned ego; not the ideal science

of pure logic, or any of the idealizations of theoretical knowledge; in short nothing is assumed, and as a beginning there is only the self-validating cognitive experience itself.[4]

But neither are such entities doubted, for this would be a negative presupposition. The aim of phenomenology is to suspend all such questions while turning to the content of consciousness itself—to the phenomena— and to see philosophy's task as being that of describing the essences of phenomena, the explication of the various levels of meaning of phenomena, and their interrelationships. Such is the significance of phenomenology's quest for a starting point free from presuppositions.

THE INTENTIONALITY
OF CONSCIOUSNESS

To refer to consciousness as *intentional* is another way of saying that consciousness is always directed toward an object. One way this is frequently put is that consciousness is consciousness of . . . (the ellipsis here indicating any possible object of consciousness). The intentional structure of consciousness is usually associated with the nineteenth-century philosopher, Franz Brentano, for whom intentionality was that characteristic of psychic or mental phenomena distinguishing them from nonmental phenomena. For Brentano, the intentionality of consciousness was primarily of psychological importance. But as appropriated by Edmund Husserl, the notion of intentionality took on a far vaster significance which placed it at the very heart of phenomenology as Husserl conceived it. For Brentano intentionality was a causal relationship to the external, concrete characteristics of things. For Husserl intentionality was not a causal relationship to objects but an activity of consciousness which is identical with the meant object.

This interpretation of the intentionality of consciousness destroys any possibility of viewing consciousness as empty or closed in upon itself. Descartes, who was searching for an absolutely undeniable point of departure on which to construct his philosophic system, found this indubitable truth in the thinking self: "I think, therefore I am" *(cogito ergo sum)*. Descartes' *cogito* was an attempt to provide an absolutely certain foundation for philosophy. But inasmuch as Descartes at this point had doubted the reality of the physical world, he was left with a *cogito* that was empty, a mere thinking thing *(res cogita)* with no guarantee that there was anything to think about. The notion that consciousness is

4. Farber, "The Ideal of a Presuppositionless Philosophy," in *Phenomenology*, edited by Kockelmans, pp. 37–58. *See* no. 118.

intentional overcomes this Cartesian dilemma, for consciouness is always consciousness *of* something. Husserl seized upon the significance implied by the recognition that consciousness is always directed toward an object: there is an indissoluble unity between the conscious mind and that of which it is conscious.

The intentionality of consciousness also points up the absurdity of dividing up reality into such mutually exclusive categories as minds and bodies, subjects and objects, and so forth. The difficulty encountered by philosophy, ever since Descartes made these distinctions, is to explain any interaction between these two kinds of reality. This problem led philosophy since the seventeenth century down some curious paths. Descartes himself attempted to explain the interaction of mind and body as occurring in the pineal gland. More serious were the attempts of later thinkers to overcome this Cartesian dualism simply by eliminating one of the terms. Idealism claimed to be able to account for reality perfectly well only in terms of mind; naturalism claimed to account for mental reality in nonmental terms. But the recognition that consciousness is intentional implies that such distinctions are misdirected. An unknowable reality, if not contradictory, is unthinkable; a completely empty consciousness closed in upon itself is inconceivable.

Another implication of the intentionality of consciousness is that it shifts the emphasis from the question of the reality of the world to the meaning of that which appears to consciousness. All questions about the reality of the world are suspended, put out of question for the moment. Once consciousness is extricated from naturalistic psychological biases, the problem of getting out into the "real" world is eliminated. The intimate connection between consciousness and the content of consciousness is then fully manifested, for consciousness is never empty and abstract but concrete and tied to the world of experience.

REFUSAL OF THE SUBJECT-OBJECT DICHOTOMY

As was mentioned above, the intentional structure of consciousness implies that all thinking is thinking about something, that every *cogito* intends a *cogitatum*. The approach of phenomenology overcomes the distance between consciousness and its content by showing the impossibility of making a radical distinction between them. The world is no longer a problem, as it was for Descartes, who was forced to develop intricate proofs for the reality of physical objects. Phenomenology, by shifting attention from the question of the reality of the world to its meaning as phenomena, overcomes the distance between the *cogito* and its *cogitatum*. Consciousness is unified, but within this unity there are the two poles of the *cogito* and its content, the *cogitatum*. The importance of this distinction for clearing up some of the confusions generated by the subject-object dichotomy is summed up by the French philosopher Pierre Thévenaz who says that

> to make the world appear as phenomenon is to understand that the being of the world is no longer its existence or its reality, but its meaning, and that this meaning of the world resides in the fact that it is a *cogitatum* intended by the *cogito*.[5]

To understand the significance of this insight is to grasp the shift from the ordinary, commonsense view of the world to the phenomenological point of view for which the world appears as phenomenon. But this leads away from a discussion of the general features of phenomenology into an examination of the phenomenological method. For if phenomenology is recognizable as a distinct philosophical movement, it is not because it has propounded a new set of doctrines but because it offers a new way of doing philosophy. For an adequate understanding of this method, it is best to begin at the beginning—with Edmund Husserl, acknowledged to be the founder of phenomenology and the principal figure in the development of the phenomenological method. A more detailed discussion of this method, and the historical context in which it arose, is the subject of the next chapter. But first a brief word about Husserl himself.

Edmund Gustav Albrecht Husserl (1859-1938) was originally trained as a mathematician at the universities of Leipzig, Berlin, and Vienna. From the latter institution he received a doctoral degree in mathematics in 1883, his dissertation being on the calculus of variations. At Vienna he came into contact with the noted philosopher and psychologist Franz Brentano, who turned Husserl's attention to philosophy. As a young *privatdozent,* Husserl first taught at the University of Halle under the philosopher Carl Stumpf. In 1900 he accepted a chair of philosophy at Göttingen, and in 1916 moved to the University of Freiburg, where he taught until his retirement in 1930. After an initial book on mathematics (*Philosophie der Arithmetik,* published in 1891), Husserl turned almost entirely to philosophy. By the second decade of the twentieth century, Husserl was increasingly recognized for his philosophical work, and from 1913 until the year of his retirement, he and several coworkers[6] produced a series of volumes dealing with phenomenological philosophy entitled *Jahrbuch für Philosophie und Phänomenologische Forschung.*

5. Thévenaz, "What Is Phenomenology?" *See* no. 9.
6. Moritz Geiger, Alexander Pfänder, Max Scheler, Oscar Becker.

Although by the time of his death Husserl had published half a dozen major books and a host of journal articles, had served as editor of the *Jahrbuch,* and was the recognized leader in phenomenological research in Europe, these facts themselves do not give a true estimate of his productivity. Unpublished were more than forty thousand pages of manuscripts, as well as seven thousand pages of transcriptions worked out by Husserl's assistants.[7] That Husserl's manuscripts survived at all is due to his coworkers, whose efforts seem even more courageous when viewed against the background of the apocalyptic events that were descending on Europe in the late 1930s. Being a Jew by ancestry, Husserl was hindered in his later years by the restrictions placed on Jews during the opening years of Hitler's regime. The library at Freiburg was closed to him, and he was able to continue his work only because his students braved the possibility of Nazi reprisals by bringing him books. Had Husserl lived longer, his fate would no doubt have been the same as millions of other European Jews.

After Husserl's death, his closest associates realized that the Nazis intended to destroy every vestige of Jewish scholarship and that Husserl's manuscripts would not survive unless they were removed from the country. This was accomplished through the aid of a group of German nuns who smuggled Husserl's manuscripts in their luggage to the Belgian ambassador in Berlin, who sent them by diplomatic courier to the University of Louvain, where they remained safe. After the war the Husserl archives were set up at that same university.[8]

The development of Husserl's thought can be divided into four distinct stages. The first was his investigations into the foundations of logic. Having been trained as a mathematician, Husserl's initial publications were in mathematics and logic. In these works he attempted to account for the foundations of logic in terms of psychology—a view shared by many of Husserl's contemporaries. This attempt proved to be unsuccessful and led him to the second stage in his development, which consisted of two aspects: (1) the rejection of the explanation of logic in terms of psychology, and (2) the development of the method known as the phe-

---

7. That transcriptions were necessary was due to Husserl's practice of writing in a shorthand of his own devising, which only a limited number of his coworkers were able to decipher. The task of editing these manuscripts is still an ongoing project that has fallen largely on the shoulders of two of Husserl's students and coworkers, Eugen Fink and Ludwig Landgrebe. The publication of Husserl's works has been undertaken by the Dutch publishing firm of Martinus Nijhoff, which has thus far issued twelve volumes under the series title Husserliana (*see* nos. 12–23).

8. An account of the preservation of Husserl's manuscripts and the establishment of the Husserl Archives at Louvain is given by Van Breda in *Husserl et la pensée moderne. See* no. 103.

nomenological reduction by which all empirical irrelevancies are excluded.

The third stage represented a further extension of the phenomenological method in an attempt to develop a science of essences, or an *eidetic* science. Although this period was the most fruitful for Husserl, in the sense that most of his publications dealt with eidetic phenomenology, it was the most controversial aspect of his work. Many of his coworkers found eidetic phenomenology to be too idealistic and questioned it in terms of the immediately experienced world. Husserl's response to his critics was to reaffirm the nonidealistic thrust of his method, and it led him to a fourth and final stage in his philosophy—the significance of the lived-world. The lived-world, the world of ordinary, immediate experience, was always in the background of Husserl's investigations, and in his fourth stage he turned directly to its explication. This emphasis in Husserl's later writings on the lived-world proved to be highly significant for the work of subsequent phenomenologists and is the direct link between phenomenology and existential philosophy. In the following chapter, the discussion of Husserl's philosophy will follow this thematic outline and will explicate each of the four stages in more detail.

Scarcely half a century has elapsed since phenomenology became a recognizable philosophic movement in Europe. It is still too early to assess fully the total impact of phenomenology and the place of Husserl in its development. But whenever the final verdict is made, there is little question that Edmund Husserl, due both to the genius of his insights and his influence on subsequent philosophy, will be regarded as one of the philosophical giants of the twentieth century.

BIBLIOGRAPHY

The works listed here offer a general account of phenomenology and for that reason provide a valuable starting point for the interested reader. By and large they do not discuss the more detailed aspects of phenomenology, nor do they assume a wide familiarity with the technical terminology employed by writers in the field.

1. Alexander, Ian W. "What Is Phenomenology?" *Journal of the British Society for Phenomenology* 1 (1970):3.

    A discussion of the general themes of phenomenology in clear and concise terminology.

2. Cairns, Dorion. "Phenomenology." In *History of Philosophical Systems*, edited by Vergilius Ferm, pp. 353–64. Paterson, N.J.: Littlefield, Adams, 1961.

A concise introduction to phenomenology articulating basic themes and emphasizing Husserl's contribution to the movement.

3. Kockelmans, Joseph J. *A First Introduction to Husserl's Phenomenology.* Pittsburgh: Duquesne Univ. Pr., 1967.

A guide to Husserl's thought written for the individual not thoroughly familiar with phenomenology.

4. Landgrebe, Ludwig. *Problems in Contemporary European Philosophy.* Translated by Kurt F. Reinhardt. New York: Frederick Ungar, 1966.

A thoroughly readable account of phenomenology's application to such basic topics as the nature of man, his relationship to the world, and his attitude toward science and religion.

5. Lauer, Quentin. *Phenomenology: Its Genesis and Prospect.* New York: Harper & Row, Harper Torchbooks, 1958.

A reprint of a work originally published as *The Triumph of Subjectivity* (New York: Fordham Univ. Pr., 1958).

6. Merleau-Ponty, Maurice. *Phenomenology of Perception.* Translated by Colin Smith. London: Routledge & Kegan Paul, 1962.

See especially the Preface, pp. vii–xxi, which is often reprinted in anthologies under the title "What Is Phenomenology?" An excellent introductory statement of phenomenological themes by one of France's leading contributors to the phenomenological tradition.

7. Ricoeur, Paul. "Sur la phénoménologie." *Esprit* 21 (1953):821–38.

A discussion of various senses the term *phenomenology* has had in the philosophic tradition with particular attention to its use by Husserl and his successors.

8. Schmitt, Richard. S.V. "Phenomenology." In *The Encyclopedia of Philosophy,* edited by Paul Edwards, 6:135–51. New York: Macmillan & Free Pr., 1967.

A lucid, concise, yet thorough discussion of the origins of phenomenology, its major emphases, and its subsequent development.

9. Thévenaz, Pierre. *What Is Phenomenology? And Other Essays.* Edited by James M. Edie. Translated by James M. Edie, Charles Courtney, and Paul Brockelman. Chicago: Quadrangle, 1962.

The title article, which first appeared in 1952 in *Revue de théologie et de philosophie,* is a discussion of the phenomenology of Husserl and its subsequent modification by Heidegger, Sartre, and Merleau-Ponty.

10. Welch, E. Parl. *The Philosophy of Edmund Husserl: The Origin and Development of His Phenomenology*. Columbia Univ. Pr., 1941. Reprint. New York: Octagon, 1965.

Contains a lucid exposition of Husserl's phenomenology and an excellent bibliography of works on phenomenology in languages other than English, reflecting the fact that at the time of its original publication, little had been written on the subject outside of Europe.

11. Zaner, Richard M. *The Way of Phenomenology*. New York: Pegasus, 1970.

Phenomenology presented as a way of philosophizing with particular attention to the phenomenological method and basic themes of phenomenological analysis.

CHAPTER 2

HUSSERL AND THE PHENOMENOLOGICAL METHOD

Edmund Husserl, the motive force in the development of phenomenology, has remained the philosophic mentor to subsequent phenomenologists. Although he did his major work in the twentieth century, the problems with which he wrestled were bequeathed to him by the philosophers of the nineteenth century, and they, in turn, were the questions that have dominated Western thought since the time of the seventeenth-century thinker René Descartes. Descartes is frequently mentioned in Husserl's works; indeed one of his later works was specifically entitled *Cartesian Meditations* and for good reason. Descartes was the watershed of all modern philosophy. His bold scheme was to bring the same kind of certainty to philosophy that characterized the mathematics of his day; his method was the now famous "Cartesian doubt."

Descartes' questions are still our questions: How can we have *certain* knowledge of the world, of the self, of God? What rational justification can we give for this knowledge? Descartes' answers to these questions, however, created more problems than solutions and set the stage for the development of philosophy during the next three hundred years. Among other things, Descartes divided reality into two poles—mind and body—and created a dualism which introduced two seemingly irreconcilable schools of philosophy, rationalism and empiricism.

This is not the place for a recapitulation of the development of modern philosophy since Descartes. But several summary statements are possible—indeed necessary—if one is to understand the context in which phenomenology arose.

Kant tried to bring rationalism and empiricism together in a new synthesis in which he attempted to find a middle ground between the two schools. But his solution contained a major ambiguity—the unknown and unknowable thing-in-itself. The resolution of this ambiguity was left to German idealists, and most notably to Hegel. It is one of the ironies of the philosophic tradition that Kant, who at all costs wanted to avoid idealism, set the stage for one of the most idealistic of all philosophers—the German thinker, Hegel.

Hegel was the first to make major use of the word *phenomenology,* but he meant by it something vastly different than what the term meant for Husserl. For Hegel, the term *phenomenology* referred to the process of the development of absolute mind. The absolute mind comes to self-awareness through successive stages in which all reality is accounted for; in short, all reality *is* mind. Consciousness and self-consciousness are merely stages in the process of the unfolding absolute. Hegel's "phenomenology of mind" did have the merit of overcoming Cartesian dualism and avoiding the Kantian ambiguity of the thing-in-itself. But its major defect was the explaining away of natural reality by making all reality ideal. Hegel's philosophic system left no room for the individual as a unique, willing, choosing, conscious being. The individual is merely one stage in the unfolding of the absolute and is even unaware that he is a tool of the absolute's coming-to-self-awareness.

NINETEENTH-CENTURY BACKGROUNDS

The nineteenth century witnessed a fierce reaction to Hegel and the rigid systematization of philosophy. Kierkegaard, most notably, protested the loss of the individual, existing person and the absence of any significant meaning of transcendence. He likened the Hegelian system to a magnificent castle unfit for human habitation. Within the system the individual cannot be a responsible, choosing, existing being; in fact, such a system excludes the question of existence completely and eliminates God as a transcendent reality in which man's being is rooted. This Kierkegaardian emphasis upon the existing individual and his relationship to transcendence became a prominent theme in certain existential philosophies a century later.

By the beginning of the twentieth century, philosophy was no longer looked upon as a discipline whose function was to supply foundations for science and, indeed, all other human endeavors. Philosophy was not seen as having any power of its own to question the assumptions of science, and its realm was narrowed to include only an explication of the meaning of logic and language. *Scientism* was one of the terms phenomenologists used to describe the elevation of science as the supreme method for resolving all human questions. Its philosophical corollary was *positivism,* with its verifiability principle, which was alluded to in the previous chapter (*see* p. 6). But positivism, even in its evangelistic fervor, failed to answer the question of the objective validity of logic itself, and it was forced into the embarrassing position of being unable to justify its own assumptions and first principles.

Thinkers of the late nineteenth century were concerned with the question of the foundations of logic, although it should be noted that the logic under question was not the contemporary formal calculus embodying Boolean notation but rather the kind of logic represented by the work of John Stuart Mill. Logic in this sense was an analysis of the basic principles, axioms, and concepts operative in reasoning processes. The overriding question was how these principles could be accounted for, and the prevailing explanation was that they could be explained in terms of psychic processes. If one understood these psychic processes, he would then be able to account for the foundations of logic. Since the investigation of the psyche was considered the proper domain of the newly formed "science" of psychology, most philosophers (Husserl included) simply assumed that the foundations of logic could be accounted for in terms of psychological "laws."

This view, referred to as *psychologism,* denied that logic had any inner dynamic; rather, logic was only the lawful functioning of certain physico-chemical processes occurring in the human brain. This means that the basic logical axioms, such as the principle of contradiction, have only empirical, not universal, validity. But since science is based on logic, a further implication of psychologism was to undercut the validity of science itself, although science was not fully aware of the dire consequences of this methodological assumption.

Another way of stating the same problem is to see that the emphasis in all rational endeavors was shifting to what are called empirical statements, that is, statements which are open to verification or falsification by an "objective" method of investigation. Even psychology was reshaped by these assumptions. The study of mental activity was reduced to descriptions of empirically describable processes; those aspects of mind not open to such analysis were deemed merely "subjective" and of no scientific importance. The effect of this shift in method was to describe the total human subject as just another "thing" in nature. Man was interpreted as another "object" to be investigated by the same methods used in the physical sciences. This signaled a kind of radical reductionism in which all human functions were reduced to physically observable characteristics. Psychology was moving toward behaviorism, a study of scientifically verifiable and measurable characteristics.

But behaviorism introduced a further paradox: although the task of psychology is to describe human behavior, the describer, who is conscious of that behavior (or even the originator of it) is left unaccounted for. By attempting to explain all mental or "spiritual" (in the sense of the German word *Geist)* phenomena in terms of physical processes, psychology reduced thoughts to physical processes, secretions of the brain, which in principle were to be explained by chemical or physiological laws. The objections made by the phenomenologists to this kind of reductionistic psychology were not objections to the empirical method as such but to the assumptions on which it was based. In its attempt to describe the total human subject in completely quantitative terms, psychology had eliminated the importance of human consciousness itself. But additionally, it led to further difficulties. If logic can be accounted for by psychology as merely a psychophysical process (presumably occurring in the human brain), then there is no criterion to distinguish one such process (the one occurring in my brain) as logically superior to another process (the one occurring in your brain). All thinking processes, including contradictory ones, would have to be viewed as equally valid if a strictly psychologistic interpretation of logic is assumed, for logic can produce no criteria by which true statements can be distinguished from false ones. But inherent in all this was a curious but devastating contradiction: while implicitly denying that truth or falsehood were terms with universal validity (how could a proposition be universally true or false if it was explainable merely as a psychical process?), psychologism was inadvertently denying the truth of its own position.

HUSSERL'S REACTION

Edmund Husserl, having been born in the second part of the nineteenth century, witnessed the breakdown of philosophy as an independent discipline. The entire intellectual climate concerning the foundations of philosophy—indeed of thought itself—was shifting toward nihilism, most dramatically portrayed in the writings of Nietzsche, the poetry of Rainer Maria Rilke, and the novels of Franz Kafka. It is, therefore, not surprising that Husserl chose mathematics, rather than philosophy, as his academic vocation. His first book, *Philosophie der Arithmetik* (1891), was an attempt to explain the basis of logic and mathematics on psychologistic assumptions. But this attempt (which Husserl later acknowledged as a complete failure) raised further disturbing questions concerning the assumptions on which psychology was based. To deal with these problems, especially in the light of a devastating critique of his book by the noted mathematician Frege, Husserl decided to investigate again the entire question relating to the foundations of logic. This he did in a work entitled *Logical Investigations*. Here one can see Husserl's abandonment of psychologism.

In the first place, Husserl pointed out that logic is presupposed by all rational attempts to deal with objective nature. How could psychology —one of the latest and most inexact sciences—claim to provide the foundations of logic, particularly when it makes use of logic in its own investigations? Additionally, psychology deals with the laws of the psyche as they are, whereas logic deals with thinking as it ought to be. In other words, Husserl viewed logic as a normative science, whereas psychology is merely empirical and descriptive. To show the absurdity of psychologism, Husserl used the Aristotelian method of reductio ad absurdum. For example, let one assume that psychology is the basis of logic. What are the consequences? Psychological "laws" are vague generalizations without exactness or certitude. It follows that logic, if based on psychology, must also be an inexact science; yet the opposite is the case. One finds that logical precepts are exact; therefore, the rules of deduction and inference cannot be mere empirical generalizations.

But assume the opposite, namely that the "laws" of psychology are exact. Since psychological procedures are empirical (i.e., based on experience), logical laws are at best empirical generalizations, with greater or lesser probability. But the general view of logic is that its principles (e.g., the principle of contradiction) are true universally and a priori. The principle of contradiction is not based on facts but prescribes the way one ought to think about facts.

Although Husserl admitted that minds are a condition for logic, he rigorously demonstrated that logic cannot be reduced simply to mental processes or understood as merely a mental creation. The objectivity of logic, according to Husserl, can be seen in that we judge the correctness of mental processes by logic; logic validates thought processes, not vice versa. Additionally, logical laws are not about any particular fact or any particular thinking subject; they are applicable to all things and to all thinking subjects. This is another way of saying that logic does not *describe* the way men do in fact think but *prescribes* to them how they must think if they wish to think logically. Of course, one must presuppose psychological activity as a condition of knowledge of logical laws, but this psychological activity must not be confused with the basis and ground of such logical thought.

In short, there is a difference between causal principles that describe the way things operate in nature and logical laws which do not presuppose nature. For example, trees do not grow logically, but in accordance with mechanical, causal laws which can be described by natural science. But when one thinks about a tree, he must think about it logically. A tree cannot both be and not be at the same time and in the same respect (the principle of contradiction), or what one calls a tree must either be a tree or not a tree (the principle of excluded middle). In the preceding discussion, the term *law* has been used in three different ways: (1) causal law, derived from empirical generalizations; (2) psychological law, such as the principle of association, ultimately derivable from empirical generalizations; and (3) logical law, which is not derived from any empirical fact, be it natural or psychological.

In line with the best of Greek philosophical tradition, Husserl recognized that objects in nature are continually changing; coming into being, growing, and passing away characterize all natural objects. But the laws which govern these changes are themselves unchanging. If this were not the case, if scientific laws were based only on empirical observation, then the laws of science would change along with the objects they describe.

Not only did psychologistic assumptions undermine the validity of science, they also opened the way to ethical *relativism* and *nihilism*. Relativism, simply described, is the view that all norms and values are of equal validity, and nihilism is the assertion that there are ultimately no norms or values. If truth is simply an "all-too-human perspective," as Nietzsche put it, then truth is simply a name given to the mental operations of a particular species, homo sapiens; or indeed, truth is only what goes on in the psychic processes of each individual person. For example, for a person to enunciate the principle of contradiction would be analogous to his announcing, "I have a headache." Both are private, internal experiences which give rise to a certain vocal response. But if a person were to say, "I have a headache and I don't have a headache," one would be unable to say (given psychologistic assumptions) his statement was false even though he had contradicted himself. To say that such a statement is false requires that logic be viewed as *prescribing* how one ought to think, not *describing* in fact how one thinks. Psychologism also leads to a further contradiction: if each person has his own truth (just as he has his own headache), then there is no truth for all men for all times. But to say that there is no truth involves one in absurdity, for it presupposes at least one truth, namely, that there is no truth.

What Husserl saw clearly in his repudiation of psychologism and relativism was that nothing less than the foundations of science itself were at stake. All sciences (in the sense of all rational endeavors) presuppose logic and the hope that truth can be found. But if logic is not secure, then nothing is. What was needed was an investigation into the basis of human knowledge itself. Thus, Husserl was led in his search for the foundations of logic from mathematics to psychology, and finally, to philosophy.

RETURN TO THE
CARTESIAN REVOLUTION

Husserl's philosophical quest began with a search for first principles. He would have entitled his work *archaeology* (from the Greek word *archē*, "origin" or "beginning," and *logos,* "reason" or "thought") had this term not already been appropriated by one of the social sciences. What was needed was a return to the best of the classical and critical philosophical tradition. In this effort, comparison with Descartes was inescapable, for the parallels between Husserl and Descartes are striking. Both were trained as mathematicians. Both were profoundly disturbed by the degraded state of philosophy in their day, with its attending skepticism. And both were searching for a basis for thought which would provide certainty and indubitability.

But there was a major difference: Husserl was convinced that Descartes had made a turn fatal to philosophy by introducing into philosophy the radical distinction between thinking substance *(res cogitans)* and extended substance *(res extensa),* or mind and nature as they were later called. Once a distinction is introduced between the mind and the object of thought, the question that then arises is how the two are to be related.

Another significant difference between Descartes and Husserl was the role played by mathematics in the thought of each. Descartes lived in the secure world of the sixteenth and seventeenth centuries when mathematics was just beginning to demonstrate its certitude and its value for the new science and astronomy. It seemed to provide a model of clear and distinct rational activity which philosophy would do well to imitate. Thus, he searched for the absolutely certain first truth on which all philosophy could be based and found it in the indubitable assertion, *cogito ergo sum* ("I think, therefore I am"). For Descartes the "I think" would serve the same function for philosophy that the axioms of logic served for mathematics. But in Husserl's time even the axioms of mathematics had been placed in question. Husserl saw that the basis for certitude which philosophy lacked had to be gained by going back of any methodology or science—be it mathematics or logic—in spite of how certain its professed certitude appeared to be. The same basis that would provide certainty for philosophy would do likewise for mathematics and natural science.

There was also the matter of Cartesian doubt. By systematically doubting the existence of the world, Descartes thought he had found a method whereby he could arrive at something which he could not doubt—namely the fact that he was doubting, which itself is a kind of thinking. Hence, that he was thinking was an indubitable fact. Although Husserl was inspired by Descartes' method of universal doubt, he charged that the way Descartes employed it was unsatisfactory because it was not radical enough. For in doubting the existence of particular things (i.e., that he was sitting by the fire, in a particular room, at a particular time, etc.) Descartes was actually operating within a framework of belief in the existence of the world. One can only doubt particular objects in the world—or particular perceptions of the world—if one believes there is a world to be doubted. Even if Cartesian doubt were followed out rigorously, it would result in a negative judgment, a denial of the world.

What Husserl proposed was a new method wherein the world would not be doubted but would be seen from a radically altered viewpoint. What this means in specific terms will be discussed below. Husserl further criticized Descartes for concluding his program of methodic doubt with the conviction that he was an existing, thinking substance (the *cogito*). This he never doubted or called into question. His problem then was to explain how thinking substance *(res cogitans)* is related to nonthinking substance *(res extensa)*. This produced what Whitehead called the bifurcation of nature, and the whole task of modern philosophy has been an attempt to overcome this division.

TO THE THINGS THEMSELVES

Husserl called for a return to the spirit of Cartesianism with an avoidance of Cartesian assumptions. It called for a new method which would provide a radically altered perspective on the world. What this radically altered perspective meant was a return "to the things themselves," as Husserl put it. What did Husserl mean by *things (Sachen)?* His answer was that a *thing* is a phenomenon, that is, anything of which one is conscious. Anything of which one can be conscious is a legitimate area of philosophic concern. Instead of trying to explain minds in terms of matter, or vice versa, Husserl demanded that each experience must be taken in its own right as it shows itself and as one is conscious of it. When a person is conscious of a table in a room, or a mathematical theorem, both are things of which he is aware and must be taken as they appear to consciousness. Obviously one would want to make a distinction between the kind of reality that belongs to a table on which he is writing and a mathematical theorem of which he is thinking. But although different in kind, both are objects of consciousness and have a reality of their own irreducible one to the other. And the mental activity by means of which one knows mathematical objects (such as theorems, postulates, etc.) and the mental activity by which one knows material objects are likewise different in kind. It would be a fatal mistake to attempt to investigate mathematical entities by the same means that are appropriate for an investigation of tables, chairs, trees, and other worldly objects. Among other aspects, Husserl's method amounted to an expansion of the meaning of the term *experience*. Instead of limiting its use to those things known by means of sense perception, Husserl applied it to anything of which one is conscious. There are many different things of which one can be aware: natural objects, mathematical entities, values, affective states, volitions, melodies, moods, desires, feelings—all these are things *(Sachen)* of which one is aware. All of these things Husserl calls *phenomena*. Phenomenology, then, became a program for a systematic investigation of the content of consciousness.

Husserl's style of philosophy obviously implies a broadening of the field of investigation appropriate to the philosophical discipline. Indeed *anything* of which one is conscious is a legitimate field of inquiry for philosophy. By this ploy Husserl was going back to the original conception of philosophy developed by the Greeks as a rational investigation of all that is. This attempt to recapture the original breadth of philosophy while simultaneously providing a firm foundation for rational activity was the motivating principle of Husserl's phenomenology. That this is a return to a classical philosophical ideal can be seen from Aristotle's observation that "it is the mark of an educated man to look for precision in each class of things just so far as the nature of the subject admits."[1] In a similar way Husserl demanded that each phenomenon must be taken as it is without imposing a methodology inappropriate to the subject matter.

THE PHENOMENOLOGICAL METHOD

The Natural Attitude

There are, of course, many subject areas with which philosophy is concerned—ethics, esthetics, theory of knowledge, philosophy of science,

1. Aristotle, *Nicomachean Ethics* 1094b 24.

metaphysics, logic, cosmology, and so forth. What, if anything, do all these discrete areas of inquiry have in common? If they have nothing in common, it would be difficult to see how a single philosophical method —be it phenomenology or any other—could deal with them. Before any philosophical question is raised, however, all these diverse areas of inquiry have one obvious common property: they are part of the commonly experienced world. This prephilosophical attitude toward the world Husserl called the "natural attitude" or "natural standpoint." The man who plants his crops and reaps his harvest is not dealing with the world in any philosophical sense. It never occurs to him to question the reality of the world in which he lives or to inquire into its rational basis. In fact, the essential attitude of human life is this natural standpoint. Whenever one is conscious, he is always related to this natural world which includes matters of fact, processes, practical aspects, values, other persons, social institutions, cultural creations, and a host of other entities. He relates to this world by means of spontaneous activities, such as observing, calculating, conceptualizing, inferring, willing, making decisions among alternatives, having emotions of joy, desire, aversion, hope, and so forth. All these acts constitute his way of relating to the natural world.

Included in the natural world are inanimate objects, animals, and other persons, all of which are a part of the natural world. There is nothing startling about Husserl's description of the natural attitude; it was not so much a theory as it was an attempt to describe the relation that consciousness has to the world of ordinary experience.

> I am aware of a world, spread out in space endlessly, and in time becoming and become, without end. I am aware of it, that means, first of all, I discover it immediately, intuitively, I experience it. Through sight, touch, hearing, etc., in the different ways of sensory perception corporeal things somehow spatially distributed are *for me simply there,* in verbal or figurative sense "present," whether or not I pay them special attention by busying myself with them, considering, thinking, feeling, willing.[2]

But not only does the natural world include other beings, both animate and inanimate, it is also a world of values, obligations, and practical affairs.

The natural standpoint constitutes the most basic web of all human relationships to the world and to other persons. But one can assume a different attitude toward the world which, although presupposing the natural attitude, differs from it. One such standpoint—and a very important one—is the "scientific" attitude or, as Husserl called it, the

2. Husserl, *Ideas,* p. 101. *See* no. 29.

"theoretical" attitude. It is different from the natural attitude in that it excludes all valuational, esthetic, and practical concerns. The scientific attitude deals with objects which have material predicates; it is a relation to the world as purely objective and removed from all subjective influences. The scientist, as scientist, must objectify the nature of his field of investigation and consider it as totally detached from all human concerns. Husserl observed that the scientific or theoretical standpoint amounts to a considerably altered understanding of nature. "Nature, simply as nature, contains no values, on esthetic qualities, etc., although these would also constitute possible objects of knowledge and organized investigation."[3]

What Husserl meant can be clearly seen by contrasting the scientific attitude with the natural attitude. In the natural attitude, nature is not present as an area of scientific investigation; as part of the natural world, the individual is involved in a host of subjective relationships with the world. But in the scientific attitude, the theorizing subject performs a multitude of acts of judging, selecting, and excluding of other possible attitudes in order to constitute nature as an object of scientific investigation. The scientist, in order to investigate nature theoretically, removes himself from the natural attitude even though as a living, human being he still operates within it. But as a scientist, having adopted the theoretical attitude, he investigates nature in a neutral fashion and excludes all other relationships with which human beings are concerned. For example, in the natural attitude, the scientist is related to his wife by means of a whole gamut of human emotions, values, practical concerns, and obligations. But as a scientist, he sees her as nothing but a swarm of molecules and a collection of physical substances. The scientific attitude narrows the range of objects of possible investigation to those of one kind —namely, material nature. There is nothing dangerous in this so long as one recognizes that the scientific attitude is a narrowing of the range of human experience; the perennial temptation of the scientific standpoint, however, is to mistakenly assume that its attitude is all inclusive.

The Philosophical Attitude

Neither the natural nor the theoretical attitudes are concerned with the basic philosophical questions. As long as the sense of wonder of which Plato spoke does not arise, that is, as long as men refrain from questioning the basis of this world of experience, there is no philosophy.

---

3. Husserl, *Ideen zu einer reinen Phänomenologie und phänomenologischen Philosophie. Zweites Buch*, p. 3. *See* no. 15.

As a matter of historical record, philosophy developed when men began to view the world from a changed attitude. Philosophy developed in Greece when men began to question the world and to demand a rational explanation for it. Instead of accepting the natural world in an unquestioned way, the philosophical attitude is the demand to know the rational foundations of the world, or as Aristotle put it, it is to ask the "reason why." Husserl called this change from the natural attitude to the philosophic attitude the "phenomenological reduction."

Husserl argued that this change from the prephilosophical to the philosophical attitude involved a questioning of all one's presuppositions about the world. It is admittedly a difficult process to describe, so Husserl used many different metaphors.

The Phenomenological Reduction. It is a common mode of expression to speak of reducing a complex problem to its basic elements. This reduction involves a narrowing of attention to what is essential in the problem while disregarding or ignoring the superfluous and accidental. What one ignores when performing the phenomenological reduction is his previous prejudice about the world. By narrowing his attention to what is essential, he hopefully will discover the rational principles necessary for an understanding of the thing (or phenomenon) under investigation.

The Phenomenological Epoche. This narrowing of attention involves the suspension of certain commonly held beliefs. To describe this aspect of the shift from the natural to the philosophical attitude, Husserl used the Greek term *epochē,* which was a technical term used by the Greek skeptics to refer to a suspension of judgment. Husserl, however, was not advocating a return to skepticism but rather a questioning of presuppositions until they could be established on a firmer basis. For example, empiricism insisted that all human knowledge can be explained in terms of sense experience. This kind of presupposition must be suspended in order to examine the full range of the different dimensions of experience (dimensions which the empiricist will overlook because of his presuppositions). Indeed, only after opening oneself to all kinds of experience will a person be in a position to decide whether empiricism is a sufficient theory for explaining human knowledge.

Bracketing. Being a mathematician, Husserl also referred to the phenomenological reduction as placing the natural attitude toward the world in brackets *(Einklammerungen).* In mathematics, one brackets (or parenthesizes) a mathematical equation in order to treat it differently. By bracketing the equation, the mathematician does not eliminate it, but merely places it out of question for the present, while the larger context of the equation is investigated.

These three terms—phenomenological reduction, epoche, bracketing

—are synonymous, and Husserl uses them interchangeably. They are different metaphors which describe the same change of attitude necessary for philosophical inquiry. A detailed exposition of how Husserl expanded the phenomenological method, and the ways in which subsequent phenomenologists applied it in actual practice, will be the burden of subsequent chapters.

One of the difficulties encountered in first reading the works of Husserl and other phenomenologists is the uncommonness of the terminology employed. For this reason it is best to begin with one of the shorter works by Husserl, such as *The Idea of Phenomenology, Cartesian Meditations,* or *Ideas: General Introduction to Pure Phenomenology.* Even in these works one may be bewildered by the rather technical terms introduced. The use of such specialized terminology, however, was both deliberate and necessary. Necessary because the traditional philosophical vocabulary was fraught with all kinds of assumptions that phenomenologists were explicitly attempting to avoid. Deliberate because these new terms were attempts to lead out of the impasse in which philosophy found itself. The following bibliography, containing a listing of all of Husserl's published works as well as major commentaries on those works, covers material not specifically discussed in this chapter. But it is advisable to list all of Husserl's works together, followed by a discussion of the subsequent development in his thought in chapter 3.

BIBLIOGRAPHY

The following is a list of all of Husserl's published books in German and English and some of his major articles in both languages. A comprehensive bibliography of Husserl's journal articles, including his early treatises on mathematics, as well as the complete contents of the eleven volumes in the *Jahrbuch für Philosophie und Phaenomenologische Forschung,* are found in the bibliography in E. Parl Welch, *The Philosophy of Edmund Husserl (see no. 10).* For readers not fluent in German, ample resources for understanding Husserl are available in English translation. For the convenience of the reader, secondary sources in the European languages are listed separately from those in English.

Husserliana

A major publishing effort by the publishing firm of Martinus Nijhoff, The Hague, Netherlands, is the Collected Works of Husserl under the editorship of Herman L. Van Breda, Director of the Husserl-Archives at

Louvain. This series is far from completed, but those volumes currently in print are listed below. Inasmuch as all the volumes in this series are published by Nijhoff, only the date of publication is given.

12. Vol. 1. *Cartesianische Meditationen* und *Pariser Vorträge*. Edited by Stephen Strasser, 1950.

An explication and application of the phenomenological method to the problem of intersubjectivity and the knowledge of other persons.

13. Vol. 2. *Die Idee der Phänomenologie. Fünf Vorlesungen.* Edited by Walter Biemel, 1950.

Formulation of the epistemological problem of naturalism in terms of transcendence and immanence and an introduction to the method of bracketing.

14. Vol. 3. *Ideen zu einer reinen Phänomenologie und phänomenologischen Philosophie. Erstes Buch. Allegemeine Einführung in die reine Phänomenologie.* Edited by Walter Biemel, 1950.

Complete exposition of phenomenology in terms of its method and a theoretical analysis of the basic structures of transcendental consciousness.

15. Vol. 4. *Ideen zu einer reinen Phänomenologie und phänomenologischen Philosophie. Zweites Buch. Phänomenologische Untersuchungen zur Konstitution.* Edited by Marly Biemel, 1952.

An analysis of the constitution of different levels of objectivity and its experience: nature, life, soul, and spirit.

16. Vol. 5. *Ideen zu einer reinen Phänomenologie und phänomenologischen Philosophie. Drittes Buch. Die Phänomenologie und die Fundamente der Wissenchaften.* Edited by Marly Biemel, 1952.

An analysis of the different regions of reality and an exposition of the relationships between phenomenology and psychology and between phenomenology and ontology, with additional considerations of method.

17. Vol. 6. *Die Krisis der europäischen Wissenschaften und die transzendentale Phänomenologie. Eine Einleitung in die phänomenologische Philosophie.* Edited by Walter Biemel, 1954.

Analysis of the historical development of scientific method with its objective-prejudice and a call to return to a more basic foundation for all human endeavors in the lived-world.

18. Vol. 7. *Erste Philosophie (1923–24). Erster Teil. Kritische Ideengeschichte.* Edited by Rudolf Boehm, 1956.

An attempt to show that Western philosophy must of necessity lead to phenomenology as its ultimate outcome.

19. Vol. 8. *Erste Philosophie (1923–24). Zweiter Teil. Theorie der phäno-menologischen Reduktion.* Edited by Rudolf Boehm, 1959.

An attempt to lead the reader into phenomenology and its foundations; as the work develops, Husserl realizes that the attempt fails and is later transformed into *Die Krisis* (*see* no. 17).

20. Vol. 9. *Phänomenologische Psychologie. Vorlesungen Sommersemester 1924.* Edited by Walter Biemel, 1962.

Clarifies the difference between psychological experience and its phe-nomenological foundations and investigates the parallels as well as the differences between psychology and phenomenology.

21. Vol. 10. *Zur Phänomenologie des inneren Zeitbewusstseins (1893–1917).* Edited by Rudolf Boehm, 1966.

Analysis of the basic levels of transcendental subjectivity in terms of time-constitution and the modes of synthesis of sense-phenomena into temporal objects.

22. Vol. 11. *Analysen zur passiven Synthesis. Aus Vorlesungs und Forschungs-manuskripten 1918–1926.* Edited by Margot Fleischer, 1966.

An analysis of the receptive area of consciousness and its modalities of synthesizing phenomena such as negation, possibility, evidence, association, and affectivity.

23. Vol. 12. *Philosophie der Arithmetik. Mit ergänzenden Texten (1890–1901).* Edited by Lothar Eley, 1970.

Husserl's first major attempt to base the science of numbers on psycho-logical activity, an attempt which failed and led to his development of phenomenology.

Books by Husserl in English

Available in English translation are some of the volumes in the Hus-serliana series, as well as other works not yet included in his Coilected Works. For annotation of the translated works, see the original citation.

24. *Cartesian Meditations: An Introduction to Phenomenology.* Translated by Dorion Cairns. The Hague: Martinus Nijhoff, 1960.

A translation of the first part of no. 12.

25. *The Crisis of European Sciences and Transcendental Phenomenology: An Introduction to Phenomenology.* Translated by David Carr. Evanston, Ill.: Northwestern Univ. Pr., 1970.

Translation of no. 17.

26. *Experience and Judgment.* Translated by James Spencer Churchill and Karl Ameriks. Evanston, Ill.: Northwestern Univ. Pr., 1973.

An analysis of the foundations of predicative judgments (both individual and universal) on the prepredicative activity of transcendental consciousness.

27. *Formal and Transcendental Logic.* Translated by Dorion Cairns. The Hague: Martinus Nijhoff, 1969.

An attempt to elaborate and define the basic concepts assumed by formal logic, their order of priority and their relationships with each other, and their relation to different regions of reality.

28. *The Idea of Phenomenology.* Translated by William P. Alston and George Nakhnikian. The Hague: Martinus Nijhoff, 1964.

Translation of no. 13.

29. *Ideas: General Introduction to Pure Phenomenology.* Translated by W. R. Boyce Gibson. New York: Humanities Pr., 1931; paperback ed., Collier, 1962.

Translation of no. 14.

30. *Logical Investigations.* Translated by J. N. Findlay. New York: Humanities Pr., 1970.

A devastating critique of naturalism, empiricism, and psychologism as inadequate and self-contradictory bases for logic and science, with an analysis of the independence of meaning from all material and psychic realities.

31. *The Paris Lectures.* Translated by Peter Koestenbaum. The Hague: Martinus Nijhoff, 1964.

Translation of the Paris lectures from no. 12.

32. *The Phenomenology of Internal Time-Consciousness.* Edited by Martin Heidegger. Translated by James S. Churchill. Bloomington, Ind.: Indiana Univ. Pr., 1964.

An edited work by Martin Heidegger based on Husserl's notes, not a translation of no. 21.

33. *Phenomenology and the Crisis of Philosophy, Philosophy as a Rigorous Science,* and *Philosophy and the Crisis of European Man.* Translated by Quentin Lauer. New York: Harper & Row, Harper Torchbooks, 1965.

Translation of the lectures which Husserl subsequently expanded into book form. Not a translation of no. 17 (*see* no. 25).

*Selected Bibliography
of Articles by Husserl*

34. "Die Frage nach dem Ursprung der Geometrie als intentional-historische Problem." *Revue internationale de Philosophie* (1938):203–25.
   Analysis of the origins of geometry in terms of space constitution.

35. "Entwurf einer 'Vorrede' zu den 'Logischen Untersuchungen' 1913." *Tijdschrift voor Philosophie* 1 (1939):106–33.
   Summary of the accomplishments of *Logical Investigations* and the basic problems facing the development of phenomenology. *See* no. 30.

36. "Grundlegende Untersuchungen zum phänomenologischen Ursprung der Räumlichkeit der Natur." In *Philosophical Essays in Memory of Edmund Husserl*, pp. 305–25. *See* no. 44.
   Analysis of the possibility of space constitution in terms of bodily motion and orientation.

37. S.v. "Phenomenology." in *Encyclopaedia Britannica*. 14th ed. (1927) 17: 699–702.
   Lucid exposition of the method and aims of phenomenology.

38. "A Reply to a Critic of My Refutation of Logical Psychologism." Translated by Dallas Willard. *Personalist* 53 (1972):5–13.
   Further discussion of Husserl's arguments against psychologism.

39. "Syllabus of a Course of Four Lectures on Phenomenological Method and Phenomenological Philosophy." *Journal of the British Society for Phenomenology* 1 (1970):38–45.
   Syllabus of lectures given by Husserl at University College, London, in 1922 dealing with the methods and aims of phenomenology.

Selected Works about Husserl

The following works amplify certain fundamental concepts in Husserl's method or are discussions of some of the works cited above. They are not comprehensive discussions of the development of phenomenology. For these consult the extensive bibliography at the conclusion of chapter 3. Annotations are given only where the title does not provide a reasonable idea of the work.

ENGLISH WORKS

40. Bachelard, Suzanne. *A Study of Husserl's Formal and Transcendental*

Logic. Translated by Lester E. Embree. Evanston, Ill.: Northwestern Univ. Pr., 1968.

    A study of no. 27.

41. Ballard, Edward G. "On the Pattern of Phenomenological Method." *Southern Journal of Philosophy* 8 (1970):421–31.

42. Elveton, R. O., ed. and trans. *The Phenomenology of Husserl: Selected Critical Readings.* Chicago: Quadrangle, 1970.

    Contains articles by figures closely associated with Husserl: Oskar Becker, "The Philosophy of Edmund Husserl"; Eugen Fink, "The Phenomenological Philosophy of Edmund Husserl and Contemporary Criticism"; Walter Biemel, "The Decisive Phases in the Development of Husserl's Philosophy": Rudolph Boehm, "Husserl's Concept of the Absolute"; Hans Wagner, "Critical Observations Concerning Husserl's Posthumous Writings"; and Ludwig Landgrebe, "Husserl's Departure from Cartesianism."

43. Farber, Marvin. *Phenomenology as a Method and as a Philosophical Discipline.* Buffalo, N.Y.: Univ. of Buffalo, 1928.

44. ———, ed. *Philosophical Essays in Memory of Edmund Husserl.* Cambridge, Mass.: Harvard Univ. Pr., 1940.

    A Festschrift for Husserl by leading phenomenologists who explicate basic phenomenological themes.

45. Molina, Fernando. "Husserl: The Transcendental Turn." In *Existentialism as Philosophy,* pp. 31–52. Englewood Cliffs, N.J.: Prentice-Hall, Spectrum, 1962.

    A good exposition of the phenomenological method showing what is involved in the shift from the natural attitude to the transcendental attitude.

46. Morrison, James C. "Husserl and Brentano on Intentionality." *Philosophy and Phenomenological Research* 31 (1970):121–38.

47. Murphy, Richard T. "Consciousness in Brentano and Husserl." *Modern Scholasticism* 45 (1968):227–41.

48. Natanson, Maurice, ed. *Essays in Phenomenology.* The Hague: Martinus Nijhoff, 1966.

    Collection of essays and journal articles on a variety of subjects pertaining to Husserl's understanding of the phenomenological method.

49. Osborn, Andrew D. *Edmund Husserl and His Logical Investigations.* 2d ed. Cambridge, Mass.: Harvard Univ. Pr., 1949.

50. Palmer, Richard E. " 'Phenomenology', Edmund Husserl's Article for the

Encyclopaedia Britannica: A New Complete Translation." *Journal of the British Society for Phenomenology* 2 (1971):77–90.
A new translation of no. 37.

51. Pivčevič, Edo. *Husserl and Phenomenology*. London: Hutchinson, 1970.

52. Ricoeur, Paul. *Husserl: An Examination of His Philosophy*. Translated by Edward Ballard and Lester Embree. Evanston, Ill.: Northwestern Univ. Pr., 1967.
Articles on all aspects of Husserl's philosophy, including a discussion of the second book of *Ideen* (*see* no. 15).

53. Sartre, Jean-Paul. "Intentionality: A Fundamental Idea of Husserl's Phenomenology." *Journal of the British Society for Phenomenology* 1 (1970): 4–5.

54. Schmitt, Richard. "Transcendental Phenomenology Muddle or Mystery?" *Journal of the British Society for Phenomenology* 2 (1971):19–27.

55. Spiegelberg, Herbert. "Husserl in England: Facts and Lessons." *Journal of the British Society for Phenomenology* 1 (1970):4–15.

56. ———. "Husserl's Syllabus of the London Lectures: Notes." *Journal of the British Society for Phenomenology* 1 (1970):16–17.
Additional material relating to no. 39.

57. ———. "On the Misfortunes of Edmund Husserl's *Encyclopaedia Britannica* Article: 'Phenomenology'." *Journal of the British Society for Phenomenology* 2 (1971):74–76.

NON-ENGLISH WORKS

58. Fink, Eugen. "Operative Begriffe in Husserls Phänomenologie." *Zeitschrift für philosophische Forschung* 11 (1957):321–37.

59. ———. "Das Problem der Phänomenologie Edmund Husserls." *Revue internationale de philosophie* 1 (1938–39):226–70.

60. Lauer, Quentin. *Phénoménologie de Husserl. Essai sur la genese de l'intentionalité*. Paris: Presses Universitaires de France, 1955.

61. Lowit, Alexandre. "Sur les 'Cinq Leçons' de Husserl." *Revue de metaphysique et de morale* 76 (1971):226–36.
A discussion of nos. 13 and 28.

62. Natorp, Paul. "Husserls 'Ideen zu einer reinen Phänomenologie'." *Logos* 7 (1917–18):224-46.

63. Scherer, Rene. *La Phénoménologie des 'Recherches Logiques' de Husserl.* Paris: Presses Universitaires de France, 1967.

64. Szilasi, Wilhelm. *Einführung in die Phänomenologie Edmund Husserls.* Tübingen: Max Niemeyer Verlag, 1959.

CHAPTER 3
FURTHER
DEVELOPMENT
OF THE
PHENOMENOLOGICAL
METHOD

After the publication of *Logical Investigations* in 1901, in which Husserl showed the inadequacies of psychologism (*see* chapter 2), he had reached something of a philosophical stalemate. The question that continually thrust itself on him was what would take the place of psychologism and provide the necessary foundations for science and mathematics. Husserl's first, tentative statement of his new philosophical method was a series of five lectures which he entitled *The Idea of Phenomenology* (*see* no. 28). In these lectures he clarified the basic problem which led to his formulation of the phenomenological method in *Ideas: General Introduction to Pure Phenomenology* (*see* no. 29).

As was discussed in the last chapter, basic to the phenomenological method was the epoche, the function of which was to bracket the entire range of assumptions based on the natural attitude. Although the epoche brackets the world of natural objects, Husserl argued that one cannot bracket everything. Even after the phenomenological epoche, something remains—the ego itself. The phenomenological epoche cannot bracket human consciousness, for the very activity of bracketing assumes it. Husserl sometimes referred to this ego as the "residue" that remains after bracketing.

In order to avoid the subject-object dualism of past philosophy, Husserl referred to this ego as "transcendental consciousness" because it is neither subjective nor objective but embraces both. Husserl used the terms *cogito* ("I think") and *cogitationes* ("thoughts") to describe this polar nature of the ego, for the ego cannot be conceived apart from its conscious life. There is no *cogito* without *cogitationes;* in short, there is no consciousness without objects of consciousness. The phenomenological epoche, which reduces the natural world to transcendental consciousness (or "transcendental subjectivity" as Husserl also referred to it), opens up an area of experience which is different in kind from empirical, transitory experience. Although the being of the world may be bracketed, one's conscious experience (and the content of that experience) cannot be excluded without contradiction.

THE STRUCTURE OF CONSCIOUSNESS

Another way of understanding the meaning of *pure consciousness* is to see that for Husserl the phenomenological method of bracketing (the epoche) demands that a philosopher place himself at a distance from all previously held theories and assumptions and become a nonparticipating observer of his conscious experiences of the world. This means that he cannot base his insights on traditional or well-established theories, whether philosophical or scientific, but on an immediate insight into the phenomena themselves. For a phenomenon precisely is one's immediate experience freed from all theoretical presuppositions and interpretations. As a result of phenomenological bracketing, consciousness is purified and only phenomena remain. Analyzing the phenomena, in turn, reveals the basic structure of consciousness itself.

As Husserl points out, consciousness is *"a universal, apodictically* [absolutely certain] *experienceable structure* of the Ego" where each conscious process *" 'means' something or other* and bears in itself, in this manner peculiar to the *meant,* its particular *cogitatum."* This meaning of something is intentionality which belongs to every conscious act.

> The house-perception means a house . . . and means it in the fashion peculiar to perception; a house-memory means a house in the fashion peculiar to memory; a house-phantasy, in the fashion peculiar to phantasy. A predicative judging about a house . . . means it in just the fashion peculiar to judging . . . . Conscious processes are also called *intentional;*

but then the word intentionality signifies nothing else than the universal fundamental property of consciousness: to be conscious *of* something; as a *cogito,* to bear within itself its *cogitatum.*[1]

These quotations from one of Husserl's later works point up the importance for phenomenology of the recognition of the fact that the basic structure of consciousness is intentional—a theme that was explored in the first chapter but requires additional explication here.

To describe the basic structure of consciousness as intentional is to say that there is no such thing as consciousness closed in upon itself. Consciousness is always directed toward an object. But a word of warning is in order: the notion of a distinct subject perceiving a separate object is so firmly engrained in everyday thinking that it is difficult to see just how revolutionary Husserl's view is. For Husserl the question of how a subject gets in contact with an object is no longer a problem; there is no such thing as bare consciousness any more than there is an inexperienceable object. One way Husserl articulated this was: *ego-cogito-cogitatum;* the "I" *(ego)* is inconceivable apart from its conscious life *(cogito),* and there is no conscious life apart from the content of consciousness *(cogitatum).*

To underscore the phenomenological view of consciousness, Husserl introduced new terminology which would avoid the subject-object dualism of older philosophical views while respecting the polar structure of consciousness. The activity of consciousness he called *noesis* (from the Greek word meaning "mental perception, intelligence, or thought"), whereas the essence to which this mental activity is correlated he called *noema* (from the Greek word meaning "that which is perceived, a perception, a thought"). The adjective forms of noesis and noema are noetic and noematic. Still a word of caution is needed: the subject-object way of thinking is so ingrained in habits of thought that one would fail to understand Husserl if he identified the noetic with the subject and the noematic with the object. Husserl stressed repeatedly that noetic activity cannot be identified with psychological activity, for it deals not with psychic processes but with the meaning of those processes. Similarly, the noematic cannot be identified with the empirical object, for it deals not with the physical experience but with the meaning of that experience. This unity of meanings is another indication of the importance of the intentional structure of consciousness. The noetic-noematic structure of consciousness cannot be identified either with the subject or object (in more traditional terminology) for it is the condition for the possibility of experiencing both the subject and the object. One never finds the noetic and

1. Husserl, *Cartesian Meditations,* pp. 28–33, passim. *See* no. 24.

noematic in isolation from each other but always correlated; they are two sides of the same coin.

THE IMMANENT AND
THE TRANSCENDENT

By the activity of bracketing the natural attitude, one extricates consciousness from all the naturalistic and psychologistic assumptions which would only lead back to the unbridgeable subject-object dualism. Phenomenologically speaking, one cannot talk about the nature of reality without including reference to one's experience of that reality. Within the experience of reality one can show how the immanence of consciousness is related to the transcendence of nature, but an important terminological distinction must be made here. Husserl insisted on the distinction between *transcendent* and *transcendental.* The word *transcendental,* as Husserl employed it, has the meaning it was given by Kant and refers to the necessary conditions for experience. That which is transcendental is neither the object of experience nor the subject having the experience; it rather constitutes the conditions within which both subjective and objective experience is possible. What is the necessary condition for any experience at all? For Husserl, it was consciousness, which is presupposed by any experience whatsoever.

But as was previously pointed out, the phenomenological reduction can never bracket consciousness itself, and Husserl refers to consciousness as the "residue" remaining after the phenomenological reduction has been made. Another way Husserl referred to this residue is as the field of pure consciousness, or again using Kantian terminology, the "transcendental" ego. The ego is transcendental because it is always presupposed in the process of bracketing and in the process of experiencing both subjects and objects. But within experience one can find transcendent and immanent levels.

Immanence refers to that which is within consciousness, whereas *transcendence* refers to that to which consciousness points. Examples will clarify the importance of this distinction. An *immanent* experience refers only to other conscious acts within the same stream of experience, as when one refers to a belief still held. A belief is within the same stream of consciousness as the activity which investigates that belief; it does not point beyond itself to something else. A *transcendent* experience, in contrast, refers beyond the stream of experience to a spatio-temporal thing (still viewed as phenomenon).

But a further complexity is introduced in the case of transcendent experience when one realizes that a spatio-temporal thing is never perceived in toto but in successive and orderly perspectives (Husserl's term was *Ordnung*), or what is often referred to by other phenomenologists as the "flux" of successive appearances. Empirical phenomena are not mere appearances but appearances *of* things. Things manifest themselves in a variety of perspectives, and although there is a successive flow of empirical appearances in time, the unity of the thing remains identical through time and is grasped by consciousness. For example, I see a house. Retaining the house in conscious view, I walk around it and continue to have the consciousness of the presence of one and the same house, although my perceptions of it constantly change. The color of the house also appears in a variety of perspectives, depending on the light cast upon it, the position of the observer, and so forth. I close my eyes and open them again and have two numerically distinct perceptions of the same house and the same color. The thing perceived (the house) remains a unity in spite of the constantly changing and numerically distinct perceptions of it. One could therefore say that the thing transcends the flux of conscious experience. But the unity of this experience is a unity of meaning, a unity grounded in conscious experience of the house. Yet this unity cannot be derived from consciousness, for there is no consciousness without consciousness of . . . (in this case, consciousness of the house). Within this unity given to consciousness but not derivable solely from the discreet and limited perspectives of the house, one can analyze the various kinds of experience (perceiving, remembering, etc.) all of which are directed toward one and the same house.

The question of how experience is unified has been a dominant theme of all post-Kantian philosophy and was one of the central issues with which Husserl dealt. Husserl's solution to this problem was to point out that the transcendental ego always orients itself toward its intended object in terms of an immediate insight into the *meaning* of its intention. But the meaning of experience cannot be accounted for either in terms of the transcendental ego alone or simply with reference to the transcendent object. The meaning of experience is that into which the transcendental ego has an insight and in terms of which it unifies its process of experience. But the meaning of experience, for Husserl, is the essence of that which is experienced; in short, essence and meaning are correlative terms. Although the transcendental ego has an insight into the meaning of experience and unifies experience in terms of this meaning, the meaning itself is not clarified apart from an understanding of essences.

BEYOND
THE EPOCHE

In his efforts to clarify how unity of meaning is given to experience, Husserl was led to extend phenomenology beyond his first formulation by developing it into what he referred to as a "science of essences." It, however, was one of the most controversial areas of his philosophy and was rejected by many of his successors. We will return to this point later.

Central to Husserl's understanding of phenomenology was the conviction that the phenomenon given to consciousness is the essence of the object experienced empirically. Phenomenology insisted that although the world transcends consciousness and is different in kind from consciousness, the intentionality of consciousness (as always consciousness of . . .) allows for an intimate connection between consciousness and the world. Things are intimately knowable; Husserl held this statement not as dogma but as perfectly demonstrable. However, the unity and knowability of the world resides in the knowability of the essence of the phenomena. Husserl called this essence the *eidos,* the Greek word for "idea." But by *eidos* Husserl meant something different from the usual meaning of idea as a subjective mental process; in Husserl's use of the term, *eidos* is the essence of what a thing is. Every experience of an individual entity can be transformed into eidetic experience or eidetic intuition (*intuition* being used here in its etymological sense of "seeing into"). The object of such an intuition is the eidos, and Husserl envisioned phenomenology as becoming a science of essences or eidetic science.

In one of his last and most important works, *Experience and Judgment (see* no. 26), Husserl explored the method of achieving this science of essences, or eidetic reduction, as he often referred to it. As the term *eidetic reduction* implies, Husserl saw this as a step analogous to but not identical with the phenomenological reduction. In the phenomenological reduction (or epoche), consciousness is extricated from naturalistic assumptions. Then one is further able to reduce consciousness to its essentials by excluding all considerations not pertinent to a particular essence. In this way the eidos is describable in all its purity. Husserl's contention was that in order to deal with empirical phenomena, one must know the essence of each phenomenon. But this eidos or essence was not conceived by him as a transcendent idea in the Platonic sense, an innate idea in the Cartesian sense, or a mental construction as Kant would have it. Neither is it identical with the empirical object. Husserl spoke of the eidos as a priori, but by this he did not mean that it was supplied solely by the mind prior to empirical experience but rather that it is an ability to have an insight prior to empirical experience which is then fulfilled or "fleshed out" by experience. In short, the eidos is the "essential possibility" without which experience would be impossible.

The eidos, or essence, is both the structure and meaning of the empirical world. Or to put it in other terms, the essence constitutes the structures which are manifested by the empirical world. For example, the essence of movement is not identical with any moving object, and yet movement is experienced immediately as an essential possibility of the object. Or to give another example, contingency is immediately experienced as an aspect of the empirical world; yet contingency is not identical with any contingent object, even though all empirical objects are essentially contingent. A third example would be color. Color, as an empirical quality of an object, is transcendent; color as a psychophysiological impression is immanent; but color as an essence is a condition for the understanding of both the quality of the experienced object and the subjective experience of it. Essences are immediately perceived or intuited in the empirical phenomenon, but the empirical phenomenon is only a condition for this experience. As Husserl put it, the contingent, or particular empirical object, and the essential, are never given one without the other in experience.[2] Because the eidos, in Husserl's view, constitutes the meaning of experience, the eidetic reduction was seen by him to be an important extension of the phenomenological method. But this was a controversial step which many of Husserl's closest associates refused to follow and still constitutes a major point of disagreement among philosophers working within the phenomenological tradition.

Another way Husserl referred to the eidetic reduction was as a method of "free variation." The eidos, being the essence of a thing, can also be viewed as a prototype of other things which can be referred to the same eidos. By introducing other things of the same kind, one thereby introduces variations which can be compared to an eidos in terms of which these various things can be seen as belonging to the same type. For example, when one deals with a particular object such as a book, one not only has an empirical impression of this particular book but an insight into what the essence of a book is. Then by freely varying the perspectives of the book, and by introducing other books which are different in some respects from the first book—in terms of size, shape, weight, color, and so forth—one still retains the eidos book to which he refers all the other specific books. For Husserl, this means that the eidos was an insight into the essence of a thing and not merely a mental construct. Were this not the case, one would confuse mental activity with the content of that activity.

The development of phenomenology as an eidetic science by Husserl served to delineate his method from that of empiricism. Husserl spoke of two kinds of intuition—*sensuous* intuition and *categorial* intuition. Sensuous intuition is what many contemporary philosophers call sense data, whereas categorial intuition is the immediate, nonempirical insight into the genus, species, or structure of any possible empirical experience. For example, to perceive a table by the five senses is a case of sensuous intuition. But recognizing in the table the differences between its shape, size,

2. Husserl, *Ideas,* p. 56. *See* no. 29.

color, texture, and so forth, while simultaneously recognizing that all these distinct qualities inhere in one and the same table, is an instance of categorial intuition. In this example one could say that the sensuous intuition "fulfills" the categorial intuition. Categorial intuition is applicable to any instance of the eidos table, whereas sensuous intuition applies only to this table and fulfills the categorial intuition. Another way of characterizing the categorial intuition is to say it is an *empty signification* or an *empty intuition* which intends any and all possible tables regardless of whether these tables are the object of immediate experience. Any empirically experienced table fulfills or "fleshes out" the intention of the categorial intuition and then can be described as a "fulfilled signification." However, lest he be accused of reintroducing a dualism of the subject-object kind, Husserl always insisted that a categorial intuition was never present apart from sensuous intuition; nor is a sensuous intuition possible apart from a categorial intuition. Whenever one experiences a particular individual thing, it immediately provides a "clue" (a term Husserl used repeatedly) concerning the particular activity of consciousness pertinent to an understanding of that entity's essence.

Husserl's attempt to expand phenomenology (by means of the eidetic reduction) into a science of essences was his effort to avoid both empiricism and subjectivism. He wanted to show that essences are part of one's immediately experienced world, but he insisted that they are neither merely *mental* nor *physical* (to use more common terminology). But many of Husserl's closest associates saw in this a tendency toward idealism, and there is a considerable weight of scholarly opinion to support this interpretation. To name a few, Eugen Fink, Martin Heidegger, and Merleau-Ponty so interpreted Husserl and offered their own expansion of phenomenology in order to avoid what they felt was an idealistic move Husserl had made. Whether or not Husserl was in fact offering an idealistic interpretation of experience remains a point of continuing controversy, although it is clear that Husserl did not think that eidetic phenomenology was idealistic. The question Husserl was attempting to answer is that of the relationship between the intuition of essences and the intuition of empirical objects (intuition being used here in Kant's sense of "seeing into"). Although Husserl's solution was to show that both are always given in experience (and one is never given without the other), his insistence that there is nevertheless a distinction between them led to the problem of finding a unity between the two. This has become the ongoing task of subsequent phenomenologists.

Regional Ontologies

Husserl was convinced that the various sciences were not able to provide a foundation for the different areas they investigate, and it was his contention that an eidetic science (as he understood phenomenology to be) could clarify the basic categories assumed by each particular science. According to Husserl, each science has its own area of investigation, but it cannot furnish the justification for delineating this area from other areas of investigation by means of its own scientific methods. Before any science can be a science, it has already assumed that this area is distinguishable from other areas in which things are already known as similar, alike, different, identical, and so forth. Husserl called the area of objectivity investigated by a particular science a "region." There are many regions: physical objectivity, psychological objectivity, mathematical objectivity, and so on. What distinguishes one region from another are the regional categories which contain the a priori presuppositions by which the entities can be collected, distinguished, and understood as belonging to a particular science. These regional categories thus constitute the basic modes of intelligibility and provide the essential description of the objects of that particular science. The sciences in which the categories of a specific region are involved were called by Husserl "regional ontologies." Hence, every science investigating a specific area of objectivity must be founded in a regional ontology. Regional ontologies determine and describe the essential structures of the objects of that particular science. This meant, for Husserl, that each science, in order to justify its own operations, must purify its assumptions by means of an eidetic science.

The basic subdivisions of regional ontologies are into *formal* ontologies and *material* ontologies. A formal ontology excludes all the specific categories of a region and deals only with the formal idea (or eidos) of "object in general." In short, it deals with the conditions under which anything can be an object of man's thoughts, science, and investigation. As a basic concept, *object in general* is an essence which underlies all essences. Material ontologies, in contrast, investigate all the conditions which are presupposed by the empirical sciences, hence a material region can be called a region of empirical objectivity. It was Husserl's claim that in order to have a rational science of nature, one must first have an eidetic science of nature.

Transcendental Constitution

Basic to phenomenology is the contention that the world has no meaning apart from consciousness. But the relationship is reciprocal: consciousness has no meaning apart from the world. Consciousness is nothing apart from its objects, meaning not the empirical object but the ideal object, or better, the essence (the eidos). For Husserl the meaning of consciousness is distinct from any empirical object, and yet it is related to and constitutes the very meaning of that object. This relationship, however, is not a causal one, for things do not come ready made and impress themselves on consciousness. Things appear to consciousness in ways that consciousness experiences them, but consciousness experiences things only in ways they appear. Husserl referred to this relationship between consciousness and the world as a process of "constitution." The reason Husserl insisted upon constitution as a process is that one cannot simply experience something by merely perceiving it; experience is more complex than that. The basic experience of a material thing requires the synthesis of different phases of the experience such as perception, retention, expectation, memory, imagination, and so forth. Only in and through these experiences does the thing show its varied sides. Husserl saw the task of constitutive phenomenology as that of describing all the modes and activities of consciousness and the merging perspectives of the things to which these activities are directed and correlated. In this dual description the constitution of the particular thing becomes apparent.

As previous discussion has shown, the phenomenological description of experience uncovers many levels and regions of experience. The experienced world consists of many levels, structures, and relationships which can be described objectively by the phenomenological method. But the experience of a thing *(Sache)* demands that these levels and relationships be unified. The necessity for such unification was dealt with by Kant a century before Husserl, and in addressing the question Husserl adopted —in broad outline—Kant's solution to the problem by accepting the importance of transcendental consciousness. As was previously pointed out, the term *transcendental* in Kant (and for Husserl as well) referred to that which was a necessary condition for experience. Following Kant, Husserl saw that for there to be unity in experience, this unity must be accounted for in terms of conscious activity. This active role of consciousness is referred to as "transcendental consciousness," or "transcendental subjectivity"—that is, the active role of consciousness is a necessary condition for the unity of all experience.

The basic role of transcendental consciousness is to provide for the temporal unification of the various levels and regions of experience. The emphasis here (as in Kant) is upon the active role of consciousness; consciousness is not merely a passive receiver of impressions but an active element in providing the synthesis of these impressions into the experience of a unified object. Temporalization, therefore, is a crucial element of transcendental consciousness. For example, when one experiences a particular entity, one experiences it in terms of many characteristics—color, size, extension, location in space, and so forth. All these levels of experience cannot be accounted for as merely a succession of impressions; they must be unified in experience in such a way as to account for one's perception of an object which exhibits all these characteristics. Not only that, one experiences this object as the *same* object through a series of successive perspectives which occur in a succession of time. Yet to make the judgment that this object which I now perceive is the same object I perceived a moment ago requires an active consciousness which retains the past perspectives as belonging to the present perception of the object with an expectation that future perspectives will also belong to the same object. This means that consciousness as intentional grasps the multitude of perspectives and levels of experience as belonging to one and the same object which is held constantly in view. If there were not this active role of consciousness, experience would only be a flux of impressions with no principle of unity to explain how these impressions are experienced as a unified object.

To emphasize the active role of consciousness in this unification, Husserl referred to this activity as constitution. It is transcendental in the sense that such constitution is a necessary condition for the unified experience of particular entities. Transcendental constitution, however, is a formal capacity of consciousness. In other words, consciousness does not create the impressions or the object around which the impressions are synthesized. It rather constitutes a unity out of the multitude of impressions in terms of the experience itself. In short, transcendental constitution is the necessary prerequisite for all experience.

The Lebenswelt

Due to the fact that Husserl expended much of his energy during the later part of his life attempting to develop phenomenology as an eidetic science, many of his closest associates accused him of moving further away from the world of everyday experience. This interpretation of his work led Husserl back to an analysis of the world of everyday experience, a concern he exhibited as early as 1907 in *The Idea of Phenomenology* (*see* no. 28). It is also a theme Husserl articulated in his last book (published posthumously), *The Crisis of European Sciences* (*see* no. 25), where he analyzed the notion of the lived-world *(Lebenswelt)*.

Before any philosophizing or theorizing, one has an unshakable belief in the lived-world, the world in which we find ourselves. Throughout one's waking life, one is concerned with projects, things, other human beings, ourselves as inner-worldly beings, in such a way that none of these levels of experience seems to be isolated but is always found in contexts which expand spatially and temporally. The context in which one experiences changing things, expectations, emotions, ideas, and so forth, Husserl referred to as "horizon," and it includes time, space, the world, and surrounding entities. For example, when one perceives an object such as a tree, he experiences it in a time and a place and in distinction from other kinds of objects. And yet the tree is only understood in its context or its horizon. The perceived object then becomes a theme for the understanding of the larger context; in this sense the object thematizes its horizon.

This horizon is always given with everything that appears, and one can never totally extricate himself from it. The lived-world is the background for all human endeavors regardless of correct, mistaken, illusory, truthful, or erroneous orientations. Husserl's emphasis on the lived-world as the concrete context of all experience provided a point of departure for later existential philosophers who, while following some of Husserl's insights, moved away from transcendental philosophy to an emphasis on being-in-the-world. So significant has this movement been that a separate chapter will be devoted to it.

In his analysis of the lived-world, Husserl pointed out that the distinctions commonly used are not arbitrary but inhere in the very nature of the particular entities experienced within the lived-world. Not all objects are the same, and it is the task of philosophy to make proper distinctions. The common-sense view recognizes that men are different kinds of entities than rocks, trees, and stars, and when one shifts from the natural to the phenomenological attitude, he carries these same distinctions with him. The notion that the lived-world is the basis for the essential distinctions with which philosophy begins provides a connection between transcendental phenomenology and the commonly experienced world.

The emphasis on the lived-world in Husserl's late period has led some interpreters to suggest that the lived-world amounts to a retreat from, if not a repudiation of, eidetic phenomenology. They see eidetic phenomenology, with its concern for essences, its emphasis on transcendental consciousness, and its exclusion of the natural attitude, as a movement toward idealism. The charge of tending toward idealism was something that plagued Husserl for a major part of his working life, although he constantly repudiated such notions and insisted that transcendental phenomenology was not idealistic. *The Crisis of European Sciences* was Husserl's final attempt to lay these charges to rest by showing that all philosophizing is rooted in the distinctions operative in experience of the lived-world. But far from convincing his critics, the *Crisis* only confirmed their suspicions that Husserl indeed had been an idealist, and his emphasis on the lived-world was a radical break with phenomenology as an eidetic science.

Another interpretation of Husserl's emphasis on the lived-world is that, while made explicit in the *Crisis,* it is nevertheless implied in his earlier work. According to this interpretation, eidetic phenomenology was only an attempt to extricate consciousness from its naturalistic presuppositions and biases. By this extrication of consciousness from the naturalistic assumptions of prephilosophical reflection, the intimate intentional relationship between consciousness and the world becomes more apparent. The experience of the lived-world provides the clues which phenomenology traces out toward the intentionality of consciousness. Hence, when eidetic phenomenology deals with essences, these essences are experienced as being in the lived-world, not in a realm of ideas separate from and distinct from experience.

Whether or not the emphasis in Husserl's later work on the lived-world represents a break and retraction of his earlier eidetic phenomenology remains a controversial issue.[3] Clearly Husserl thought there was no discontinuity between these two stages in his thought, although many of his successors—who have become significant thinkers in their own right —strongly insist that there is. While a matter of scholarly interest, this controversy does not detract from Husserl's importance. For what is ultimately of value in his work is the phenomenological method, which has opened up a fruitful way of thinking for a whole generation of philosophers.

THE UNIQUENESS OF PHENOMENOLOGY

Because phenomenology is sufficiently new, it is a constant temptation for interpreters to understand it to be only a new variation on Cartesianism, Kantianism, or phenomenalism. Resultantly, much of Husserl's attention was given to clarifying his view in contrast to these other orientations which he rejected. To see the differences—as well as the similarities—between Husserl and other philosophical orientations helps in pinpointing the contributions offered by the phenomenological method.

Phenomenology and Cartesianism

Although Husserl undoubtedly felt he was continuing (but radicalizing) the work of Descartes, the method he employed was not that of Cartesian doubt. At first the epoche (or bracketing) looks like Cartesian doubt in new dress, but this is far from the case. Husserl charged that Descartes doubted only particular entities with the full assumption of the being of the world in the background. Husserl's intent was to radicalize Cartesian

3. For a discussion of these issues, *see* volume 2 of *Analecta Husserliana: The Yearbook of Phenomenological Research* (Dordrecht: D. Reidel, 1972).

doubt, but unlike Descartes he did not affirm the nonbeing of the world. The epoche is not doubting the existence of the world or being skeptical about it but is suspending judgment concerning its reality or nonreality. This bracketing of the natural standpoint does not change one's experience of the world but only helps one see it in a new light.

The purpose of bracketing is not to limit experience only to those things which are indubitable but to open up experience of the world by discarding all limiting theories and presuppositions. An additional feature of the epoche is the emphasis it places on one's own consciousness *(cogito)*. Consciousness was not conceived by Husserl (as it was by Descartes) as another thing or object in the world (a *res cogita,* as Descartes put it) but as a correlate of the world's essence. This essence can only be known by allowing one's self to be open to the full range of conscious experience, which the phenomenological epoche achieves.

Phenomenology and Kantianism

A confusion of Husserlian phenomenology with Kantian philosophy is even more tempting, for Husserl made use of much terminology first introduced into philosophy by Kant, and he was obviously indebted to Kant for his emphasis on the active role of consciousness. There are major differences, however. For example, Kant's well-known distinction between the thing-in-itself (the *Ding-an-sich*) and the phenomenal world constitutes a division that may cause some confusion when one is reading Husserl. By *phenomenon* Kant meant that which one experiences empirically; such experience, in fact, for Kant is the only avenue to any valid knowledge. Over against the phenomenon Kant set the thing-in-itself (also called by Kant the *noumenon)* which is unknown and unknowable. For Kant, one cannot say anything about the thing-in-itself—whether it is the cause of the phenomenon or its ontological ground. All attempts by reason to go beyond the phenomenon to the thing-in-itself (that is beyond empirical experience) result in logical confusion and contradiction.

In contrast, Husserl charged Kant with limiting (perhaps due to Kant's "scientific" prejudices) experience to only one kind—namely empirical experience—and ignoring other areas, such as logic and mathematics, scientific theories, values, and other "ideal" objects. Kant also fails to give a foundation for empirical experience by assuming that all mental processes are alike. For Husserl, the object given to consciousness is the essence of the object experienced empirically. Husserl insisted on the irreducibility of this essence (or *eidos*) to any subjective process, which meant that for Husserl the phenomenon that gives itself to consciousness is what Kant meant by the thing-in-itself. Husserl thereby overcame the distinction—so troubling to Kant—between the phenomenal and noumenal objects.

There is a further crucial difference between Kant and Husserl. For Kant, the unexperienced world is a chaotic succession of unstructured events. It is only when consciousness organizes this ununified flux according to its own rules that meaning arises. In other words, Kant held that the ego bestows meaning on the world in order to make sense of it. Kant referred to this as "constituting" the world. Although Husserl agreed that the world has no meaning apart from consciousness, the relationship is reciprocal: consciousness has no meaning apart from the world. Consciousness is nothing apart from essence *(eidos)* of that of which it is conscious. For Husserl, meaning is distinct from any empirical object, and yet it is related to and constitutes the very meaning of that object. One can see, too, that in Husserl's view the relationship between consciousness and the essence of consciousness is always reciprocal, whereas for Kant the synthesizing activity of consciousness was all-important. An additional difference also arises in the use of the term *intuition.* Kant used the word *intuition* to refer to one's empirical experience of the object; for Husserl *intuition* refers to one's consciousness of the essence of the empirical object (Husserl's term was *Wesenchau).*

Phenomenology and Phenomenalism

In situating Husserl and phenomenology within the context of modern philosophy, it is important to emphasize a significant difference between phenomenology and phenomenalism. Phenomenalism is a view stemming from the British empiricists and Kant, which affirms that only phenomena are knowable and that there is nothing "behind" phenomena—or if there is, it is unknowable. Phenomena are mere appearances to the perceiving subject and are combined into unities of experience by the mind of the perceiver. This position was represented in its extreme form by Berkeley, who articulated the principle, "to be is to be perceived." Although Kant affirmed that in addition to phenomena there are things-in-themselves, he denied that knowledge of them is possible, thus moving dangerously close to phenomenalism.

The German term for appearance is *Schein,* and Husserl—in order to differentiate his view from phenomenalism—spoke not of appearances but of phenomena *(Erscheinungen)* which are not mere appearances but appearances *of* something. Phenomenology views the empirical object as a correlate of conscious experience but as not identical with that experience. In other words, the empirical phenomenon is that through which the thing of which one is conscious appears. Thus, phenomenology cut a middle path between the subject-object dualism of Descartes and the idealism of Berkeley, which reduced phenomena only to states of consciousness.

Whereas there is some similarity between Husserl's empiricism and Berkeley's idealistic empiricism, these similarities are modified by Husserl's return to the full range of conscious experience. Phenomenology, for example, corrects a theory vigorously defended by the British empiricists that secondary qualities (colors, sounds, smells, tastes, etc.) are representations or images in the mind, not qualities inhering in the things themselves. Husserl, to the contrary, argued that secondary qualities are objects of consciousness which do not depend for their being on the activity of consciousness. In contrast to Berkeley, Husserl insisted that secondary qualities are not mere representations. In direct experience one does not encounter a representation or image but the spatial thing as a unity manifesting itself through a multiplicity of changing perspectives. It must be noted that a spatial thing appears in an imperfect way inasmuch as one only perceives it partially and one-sidedly. Yet there is a unity to the thing perceived, and consciousness must grasp this unity in order to make sense out of the changing perspectives of the spatial thing. Unless this unity were given to consciousness in the phenomena themselves, there would be no way for consciousness to relate the successive flux of experiences in an orderly manner. Consciousness by itself, however, cannot be the source of this unity, for in order to construct such a unity out of the flux of experiences, that unity would already have to be known. Therefore, the thing experienced is not a product of synthetic mental activity alone; on the contrary, the mental activity unifies itself in terms of the experienced unity and identity of the thing given to experience.

Phenomenology and Life-Philosophy

During the period Husserl worked, another major philosophical view developed in Germany known as life-philosophy (Lebensphilosophie). Again it is the case that some interpreters have confused Husserl's phenomenological method, with its emphasis on consciousness, as a form of this life-philosophy, particularly due to Husserl's attention to the lived-world. But such is most decidedly not the case. With the breakdown of Hegelian idealism, life-philosophy shifted the center of investigation to the empirical, changing human being. In order to give an ontological foundation for this view, its adherents introduced the concept of life as underlying all phenomena. This trend was exemplified by Nietzsche, but its greatest exponent was Wilhelm Dilthey. Husserl saw this movement as a subjective turn toward life's irrational forces, and he objected to its unfounded assumptions which themselves needed rational clarification. Husserl also criticized life-philosophy as merely psychologism in new guise, inasmuch as it attempted to reduce all human phenomena to life forces. Elsewhere Husserl objected to this kind of anthropologism (the reduction of all philosophical questions to question about man, *anthropos*) by arguing that life itself is not ultimate but is a phenomenon that can be investigated by consciousness. Husserl also pointed out that consciousness cannot be adequately understood as a function of life, as the life-philosophers would have it, but that life is a function of consciousness. A function cannot go beyond its foundations, and yet life is merely one among numerous phenomena which are open to consciousness. Hence consciousness has greater extent in functioning than life; life is limited to a particular time and place, whereas consciousness knows no such limitation. Additionally, consciousness directs life towards its goals. Without consciousness, life would have no meaning. But consciousness is not the sole giver of meaning, nor is the world meaningless. The relation between the world and consciousness is reciprocal; consciousness derives its meaning from the world, and the world derives its meaning from consciousness. The meaning of either is not given in isolation from the other.

Husserl's development of phenomenology into an eidetic science did not meet with unanimous support from his associates, as has already been mentioned. Whereas most were willing to follow his method through the phenomenological epoche and agreed with his criticisms of psychologism and all naturalistic philosophies, many were not in sympathy with Husserl's claim that phenomenology should be a science of essences. Included in this list are such prominent thinkers as Martin Heidegger, Jean-Paul Sartre, Maurice Merleau-Ponty, Paul Ricoeur, Herbert Spiegelberg, and Eugen Fink. But neither has phenomenology remained static since Husserl's time. It is a philosophic method that is continually being expanded and applied in different ways, one of the most notable of which is its adaptation by existential philosophers. All of this is in the spirit of Husserl's work, for throughout his life he attempted to clarify the phenomenological method and apply it to new areas of investigation. It was indeed his constant assertion that the phenomenological method had not been completely articulated and that further work was needed. Being totally dedicated to philosophy, even Husserl's dying thoughts centered on phenomenology. And on his deathbed he remarked, "Now I could begin."

BIBLIOGRAPHY

Although articles dealing with phenomenological philosophy and related topics have appeared in virtually all philosophical journals, several periodicals are devoted especially to phenomenology. *Philosophy and Phenomenological Research,* edited by Marvin Farber and published by the University of Buffalo since 1940, is the official organ of the International Phenomenological Society. The *Journal of the British Society for Phenomenology,* edited by Wolfe Mays, began publication in 1970, and Duquesne University established a new phenomenological journal, which began publication in 1972, entitled *Research in Phenomenology.* A new serial publication was initiated in 1971 under the title *Anelecta Husserliana: The Yearbook of Phenomenological Research,* edited by Anna-Teresa Tymieniecka (Dordrecht: D. Reidel). In the United States, the Society for Phenomenology and Existential Philosophy meets annually at various universities to discuss topics related to phenomenology. Although the society publishes no journal, many of the papers read at these meetings have appeared in various published collections (*see* nos. 110, 111, and 113).

The most extensive publishing project in phenomenology is a series of works in English, German, and French published by the Dutch firm of Martinus Nijhoff under the general title Phaenomenologica. Reflecting a variety of viewpoints, this series is sponsored by the Husserl-Archives and is under the editorship of a distinguished committee including Herman L. Van Breda (president), Marvin Farber, Eugen Fink, Jean Hyppolite (deceased), Ludwig Landgrebe, Maurice Merleau-Ponty (deceased), Paul Ricoeur, Karl Hans Volkmann-Schluck, Jean Wahl, and J. Taminiaux (secretary). Begun in 1958, the series already numbers forty-two volumes with additional titles added yearly. Because it is a separate series, all titles in this collection are listed together with no attempt to separate English from non-English works. The publisher has assigned a number (reflecting the order of publication) to each volume in the series, and it appears in parentheses following the date of publication.

Phaenomenologica

65. Aguirre, Antonio. *Genetische Phänomenologie und Reduktion: Zur Letztbegründung der Wissenschaft aus der radikalen Skepsis im Denken E. Husserls.* 1970 (38).

   Analysis of the origins of scientific concepts and their basis in transcendental constitution.

66. Biemel, Walter. *Philosophische Analysen zur Kunst der Gegenwart.* 1968 (28).

Using phenomenological method shows the different areas of aesthetic experience and their underlying structures.

67. Boehm, Rudolf. *Vom Gesichtspunkt der Phänomenologie: Husserl-Studien.* 1968 (26).
Investigates the basic phenomenological positions.

68. Broekman, Jan M. *Phänomenologie und Egologie: Faktisches und transzendentales Ego bei Edmund Husserl.* 1963 (12).
Analyzes the difference between natural and phenomenological positions; shows the constitution of the worldly ego.

69. Claesges, Ulrich. *Edmund Husserls Theorie der Raumkonstitution.* 1964 (19).
Shows the origination of space in terms of the constitution of material nature.

70. Conrad, Theodor. *Zur Wesenlehre des psychischen Lebens und Erlebens.* 1968 (27).
Analysis of psychic processes and states in terms of phenomenological method.

71. de Waelhens, Alphonse. *Le Philosophie et les expériences naturelles.* 1961 (9).
Shows the difference between philosophical thought and natural experience and the basis of philosophy in natural experience.

72. Declève, Henri. *Heidegger et Kant.* 1970 (40).
Presents Heidegger's attempt to solve Kant's ontological problem.

73. Dufrenne, Mikel. *Jalons.* 1966 (20).
Deals with philosophical questions in Spinoza, Kant, Hegel, Heidegger, Bachelard, Sartre, and Merleau-Ponty.

74. *Edmund Husserl 1859–1959: Recueil commémoratif publié à l'occasion du centenaire de la naissance du philosophe.* 1959 (4).
Contributions by leading phenomenologists concerning Husserl's life, personality, and philosophy.

75. Eley, Lothar. *Die Krise der Apriori in des transzendentalen Phänomenologie Edmund Husserls.* 1962 (10).
Discussion of the methodological problems and the paradox of subjectivity in transcendental phenomenology.

76. ———. *Metakritik der formalen Logik: Sinnliche Gewissheit als Horizont der Aussagenpolitik und elementaren Prädikatenlogik.* 1969 (31).

An attempt to show the basis of predicative logic in the perceptual world horizon.

77. Fink, Eugen. *Sein, Wahrheit, Welt. Vor-Fragen zum problem des Phä-nomen-Begriffs.* 1958 (1).
An elucidation of the questions leading to a better understanding of the concept of *phenomenon.*

78. ———. *Studien zur Phänomenologie, 1930–1939.* 1966 (21).
An analysis of the meaning of epistemological representations and an evaluation of Husserl's philosophy in light of his critics.

79. Frings, Manfred. *Person und Dasein: Zur Frage der Ontologie des Wert-seins.* 1969 (32).
Shows the similarities as well as differences between Scheler and Heidegger in terms of value questions.

80. Geraets, Theodore F. *Vers une nouvelle philosophie transcendentale. La Genèse de la philosophie de Maurice Merleau-Ponty jusqu'à la phénom-énologie de la perception.* 1970 (39).
Shows the origins of Merleau-Ponty's philosophy in transcendental phenomenology and reasons for Merleau-Ponty's rejection of it.

81. Held, Klaus. *Lebendige Gegenwart: Die Frage nach der Seinsweise des transzendentalen Ich bei Edmund Husserl, entwickelt am Leitfaden der Zeitproblematik.* 1966 (23).
An analysis of the areas of experience which are self-creative and motivated in terms of time constitution.

82. Husserl, Edmund. *Briefe an Roman Ingarden: Mit Erläuterungen und Erinnerungen an Husserl.* Edited by Roman Ingarden. 1968 (25).
Husserl's letters to Roman Ingarden showing many insights into Husserl's personality.

83. Janssen, Paul. *Geschichte und Lebenswelt: Ein Beitrag zur Diskussion von Husserls Spätwerk.* 1970 (35).
Discussion of the problem of relating transcendental phenomenology to history and the lived-world and the problem of basing history in the lived-world.

84. Kern, Iso. *Husserl und Kant: Eine Untersuchung über Husserls Verhältnis zu Kant und zum Neokantianismus.* 1964 (16).
Analysis of Husserl's relationship to Kant and neo-Kantianism and the difference between phenomenology and Kantianism.

85. Laffoucrière, Odette. *Le Destin de la pensée et "la mort de Dieu" selon Heidegger.* 1968 (24).

Discussion of the problem of the "death of God" in Heidegger and the possibilities of developing the notion of God in terms of being.

86. Levinas, Emmanuel. *Totalité et infini: Essai sur l'exteriorité.* 1961. 3d ed. 1968 (8).

Presents a phenomenological ontology in terms of the various dimensions of human existence and its relation to transcendence. Available in English as *Totality and Infinity: An Essay on Exteriority.* Translated by Alphonso Lingis (Pittsburgh: Duquesne Univ. Pr., 1969).

87. Marx, Werner. *Vernuft und Dasein.* 1970 (36).

Shows the limitations of traditional concepts of reason and develops reason in terms of logos. Translated as *Reason and World* (The Hague: Martinus Nijhoff, 1971).

88. Mohanty, J. N. *Edmund Husserl's Theory of Meaning.* 2d ed. 1969 (14).
Analysis of Husserl's concept of meaning in light of analytic philosophy.

89. ————. *Phenomenology and Ontology.* 1970 (37).

Discussion of the possibility and problems of ontology within phenomenology.

90. Piguet, J.-Claude. *De l'esthétique à la métaphysique.* 1959 (3).
Shows the metaphysical implications of esthetics.

91. Richardson, William J. *Heidegger. Through Phenomenology to Thought.* 2d ed. 1967 (13).

Shows the development of Heidegger's philosophy and its relationship to the philosophical tradition.

92. Rosales, Albert. *Transzendenz und Differenz: Ein Beitrag zum Problem der ontologischen Differenz bein frühen Heidegger.* 1970 (33).

Analyzes the problem of showing the difference between entities and Being in Heidegger's thought.

93. Roth, Alois. *Edmund Husserls ethische Untersuchungen: Dargestellt anhand seiner Vorlesungsmanuskripte.* 1969 (7).

Describes Husserl's ethical views developed within a phenomenological standpoint.

94. Saraïva, Maria Manuela. *L'Imagination selon Husserl.* 1970 (34).

An investigation of imagination in Husserl's philosophy and methodology.

95. Schuhmann, Karl. *Die Fundamentalbetrachtung der Phänomenologie: Zum Weltproblem in der Philosophie Edmund Husserls.* 1971 (42).
Analysis of world as an anonymous horizon and the methodological problems of reaching it.

96. Schutz, Alfred. *Collected Papers, I: The Problem of Social Reality.* Edited by Maurice Natanson. 2d ed. 1967 (11).
An application of phenomenological method to social reality.

97. ———. *Collected Papers, II: Studies in Social Theory.* Edited by A. Brodersen. 1964 (15).
A continuation of the studies of no. 96.

98. ———. *Collected Papers, III: Studies in Phenomenological Philosophy.* Edited by I. Schutz. 1966 (22).
An expansion and continuation of nos. 96 and 97.

99. Sinha, Debabrata. *Studies in Phenomenology.* 1969 (30).
Deals with areas in phenomenology such as logic, person, science, and ontology.

100. Sokolowski, Robert. *The Formation of Husserl's Concept of Constitution.* 1964 (18).
Investigates the various levels of constitution and their basic relationship to time.

101. Spiegelberg, Herbert. *The Phenomenological Movement: A Historical Introduction.* 2 vols. 2d ed. 1965 (5–6).
The most comprehensive survey of phenomenology available stressing origins of phenomenological method, its subsequent development, and its contemporary manifestations.

102. Thinès, Georges. *La Problématique de la psychologie.* 1968 (29).
Shows that the foundations of psychology are not within the area of natural sciences.

103. Van Breda, Herman L., and Taminiaux, J. eds. *Husserl et la pensée moderne: Husserl und das Denken der Neuzeit.* 1959 (2).
Contains articles on phenomenology in German and French translations from the second international conference on phenomenology, Krefeld, held in 1956.

104. Waldenfels, Bernhard. *Das Zwischenreich des Dialogs: Sozialphilosophische Untersuchungen in Anschluss an Edmund Husserl.* 1971 (41).
Bases the concept of social relationships on the transcendental notion of intersubjectivity.

105. Zaner, Richard M. *The Problem of Embodiment: Some Contributions to a Phenomenology of the Body.* 1964 (17).
Investigates the thesis of major phenomenologists and existentialists concerning the experience of body.

English Works

106. Aristotelian Society for Systematic Study of Philosophy. *Phenomenology: Proceedings, Supplementary Vol. II.* 1932. New York: Johnson Reprint, n.d.

107. Carr, David. "Husserl's Problematic Concept of the Life-World." *American Philosophical Quarterly* 7 (1970):331–39.

108. Chapman, Harmon M. "Realism and Phenomenology." In *The Return to Reason: Essays in Realistic Philosophy,* edited by John Wild. pp. 3–35. Chicago: Regnery, 1953.

109. Dupré, Wilhelm. "Phenomenology and Systematic Philosophy." *Philosophy Today* 13 (1969):284–95.

110. Edie, James M., ed. *An Invitation to Phenomenology: Studies in the Philosophy of Experience.* Chicago: Quadrangle, 1965.
Collection of articles dealing with epistemology, value theory, history, and special problems in phenomenological analysis.

111. ———, ed. *New Essays in Phenomenology: Studies in the Philosophy of Experience.* Chicago: Quadrangle, 1969.
Collection of articles on various phenomenological topics.

112. ———. "Phenomenology as a Rigorous Science." *International Philosophical Quarterly* 48 (1967):490–508.

113. ———, ed. *Phenomenology in America: Studies in the Philosophy of Experience.* Chicago: Quadrangle, 1967.
Articles by various authors discussing some of the current programs of phenomenological research, the tasks of phenomenology, and its application to individual and social life.

114. Farber, Marvin. *The Aims of Phenomenology: The Motives, Methods, and Impact of Husserl's Thought.* New York: Harper & Row, Harper Torchbooks, 1966.
Discussion of Husserl's development of the phenomenological method and the current reactions to and further development of the method.

115. ———. *The Foundations of Phenomenology: Edmund Husserl and the Quest for a Rigorous Science of Philosophy*. Cambridge, Mass.: Harvard Univ. Pr., 1943.
Shows the problems Husserl dealt with in *Logical Investigations* and how they led to phenomenology in vol. 1 of *Ideas* (*see* no. 29).

116. ———. "A Review of Recent Phenomenological Literature." *The Journal of Philosophy* 27 (1930):337–49.
Excellent précis of basic phenomenological themes in Husserl's work and addressed to an American audience unfamiliar with phenomenology.

117. Fulton, Street. "Husserl's Significance for the Theory of Truth." *Monist* 45 (1935):264–306.

118. Kockelmans, Joseph J., ed. *Phenomenology: The Philosophy of Edmund Husserl and Its Interpretation*. Garden City, N.Y.: Doubleday, Anchor, 1967.
Excellent collection of excerpts from Husserl's works plus articles elaborating basic phenomenological themes.

119. ———. "World-Constitution: Reflections on Husserl's Transcendental Idealism." *Analecta Husserliana* 1 (1971):11–35.

120. Lanz, Henry. "The New Phenomenology." *Monist* 34 (1924):511–27.
A discussion of phenomenology written when the movement was still in its infancy.

121. Levin, David M. "Induction and Husserl's Theory of Eidetic Variation." *Philosophy and Phenomenological Research* 29 (1969):1–15.

122. ———. *Reason and Evidence in Husserl's Phenomenology*. Evanston, Ill.: Northwestern Univ. Pr. 1971.
Contains an extensive bibliography of works on phenomenology.

123. Medina, Angel. "Husserl on the Nature of the 'Subject'." *New Scholasticism* 45 (1971):547–72.

124. Natanson, Maurice. "Phenomenology as a Rigorous Science." *International Philosophical Quarterly* 7 (1967):5–20.

125. Owens, Thomas J. *Phenomenology and Intersubjectivity: Contemporary Interpretations of the Interpersonal Situation*. The Hague: Martinus Nijhoff, 1970.

126. Pettit, Philip. *On the Idea of Phenomenology*. Dublin: Scepter, 1969.

127. Reinach, Adolph. "Concerning Phenomenology." Translated by Dallas Willard. *Personalist* 50 (1969):194–221.
Translation of lecture given originally in 1914 by a coworker of Husserl who explains the differences between phenomenology, science, and psychology.

128. Sallis, John C. "The Problem of Judgment in Husserl's Later Thought." *Tulane Studies in Philosophy* 16 (1967):129–52.

129. Schutz, Alfred. "Type and Eidos in Husserl's Late Philosophy." *Philosophy and Phenomenological Research* 20 (1959–60):147–65.

130. Smith, David Woodruff and McIntyre, Ronald. "Intentionality via Intensions." *Journal of Philosophy* 68 (1971):541–60.

131. Smith, F. Joseph, ed. *Phenomenology in Perspective.* The Hague: Martinus Nijhoff, 1970.
Collection of articles dealing with a phenomenological treatment of such topics as ethics, music, and language.

Non-English Works

132. Berger, Gaston. "L'Originalité de la phénoménologie." *Les Études philosophiques* 91 (1954):249–59.

133. Biemel, Walter. "Die entscheidenden Phasen der Entfaltung von Husserls Phänomenologie." *Zeitschrift für philosophische Forschung.* 13 (1959): 187–213.

134. ————. "Husserls Encyclopädia-Britannica-Artikel und Heideggers Anmerkungen dazu." *Tijdschrift voor Philosophie* 12 (1950):246–80.

135. Brand, Gerd. *Welt, Ich und Zeit. Nach unveröffentlichten Manuskripten E. Husserls.* The Hague: Martinus Nijhoff, 1955.
Investigates the concept of time and its origin in transcendental subjectivity based on the unpublished manuscripts of Husserl.

136. de Waelhans, Alphonso. "Die Bedeutung der Phänomenologie." *Diogenes: Internationale Zeitschrift für die Wissenschaft vom Menschen* 2 (1954): 610–30.

137. Desanti, Jean T. *Phénoménologie et Praxis.* Paris: Editions Sociales, 1963.

138. Diemer, Alvin. *Edmund Husserl: Versuch einer systematischen Darstellung seiner Phänomenologie.* Meisenheim Am Glan: Anton Hain, 1956.

139. ————. "Die Phanomenologie und die Idee der Philosophie als strenge Wissenschaft." *Zeitschrift für philosophische Forschung* 13 (1959):243–62.

140. Fink, Eugen. "Reflexionen zu Husserls phänomenologischer Reduktion." *Tijdschrift voor Philosofie* 33 (1971):540–58.

141. Landgrebe, Ludwig. "Die Phänomenologie der Leiblichkeit und das Problem der Materie." In *Beispiele. Festschrift für Eugen Fink zum 60 Geburtstag,* edited by Ludwig Landgrebe, pp. 291–307. The Hague: Martinus Nijhoff, 1965.

142. Lanteri-Laura, Georges. *Phénoménologie de la subjectivité.* Paris: Presses Universitaires de France, 1968.

143. Lowitt, Alexandre. "D'on vient l'ambiguïté de la phénoménologie?" *Bulletin de la Société Française de Philosophie* 65 (1971):3–68.

144. Seebohm, Thomas. *Die Bedingungen der Möglichkeit der Transzendental-Philosophie.* Bonn: H. Bouvier, 1962.
    Shows the problematic areas in the conception of transcendental subjectivity with an extensive bibliography concerning the notion of "transcendental subject" from Kant to 1961.

145. Stroeker, Elizabeth. "Das Problem der 'Epoche' in der Philosophie Edmund Husserls." *Analecta Husserliana* 1 (1971):170–85.

146. Vajda, Mihály. *Science entre parenthèses: Une critique de la conception scientifique de la phénoménologie de Husserl.* Budapest: Akadémiai Kiadó, 1968.

147. Van Breda, Herman L., ed. *Problèmes actuels de la phénoménologie: Actes du Colloque International de Phénoménologie.* Paris: Desclée de Brouwer, 1952.

148. Van Peursen, C. A. *Fenomenologie en Werkelijheid (Phénoménologie et réálité).* Utrecht: Spectrum, 1967.

149. Wagner, Hans. "Kritische Bemerkungen zu Husserls Nachlass." *Philosophische Rundschau* 1 (1953):1–22.
    An analysis of Husserl's late, unpublished manuscripts showing what is merely repetitious of earlier work and what is worthy of future study.

PART 2
FURTHER EXPANSION OF PHENOMENOLOGY

CHAPTER 4

EXISTENTIAL PHENOMENOLOGY

Existentialism is well known in this country both as a literary and philosophical movement, but its roots in phenomenology are not as widely understood. Historically, the roots of existential philosophy can be traced to the nineteenth-century writings of Søren Kierkegaard, Friedrich Nietzsche, and Fyodor Dostoyevsky. Central to the work of these figures was an emphasis on the existing individual, a revolt against philosophical system-building, and a call for a consideration of man in his concrete situation, including his culture, history, relations with others, and above all, the meaning of personal existence.

But it was not until the twentieth century when these concerns were wedded to the phenomenological method that existentialism became a recognizable philosophy. Failure to see this intimate connection between phenomenology and existentialism will result in thinking of existentialism as only a subjective reaction against systematic thinking and not as a philosophic movement with its own set of problems and methods. This point is well shown by the French philosopher, Paul Ricoeur, in his article on existential phenomenology for the *Encyclopédie Française*.

In it he points out the two streams that combine to produce twentieth-century existential philosophy: (1) the later works of Husserl, especially those that emphasized the *Lebenswelt* (lived-world), which focus on the universal presupposition of everyday experience; (2) the philosophies of the nineteenth century (especially Kierkegaard and Nietzsche) which revolt against all-encompassing systems. It is the confluence of these two that produced the contemporary movement known as existentialism. But Ricoeur suggests that this type of philosophy is best referred to as "existential phenomenology" because it signals a union of Husserl's phenomenological method with the concerns articulated by Kierkegaard and Nietzsche.[1] It would be accurate to say that existentialism begins where Husserl's phenomenology left off; this view is seen most clearly in existentialism's appropriation of Husserl's investigations of the lived-world.

PHENOMENOLOGY AND
THE LIVED-WORLD

Whereas Husserl saw the task of transcendental phenomenology to be that of describing the lived-world from the viewpoint of a detached observer, existential phenomenology insists that the observer cannot separate himself from the world. Existential phenomenologists followed out more rigorously the implications of the doctrine of the intentionality of consciousness. Since consciousness is always consciousness of . . . , the world is not only the correlate of consciousness but that without which there would be no conciousness. Consequently, for existential phenomenology, the modalities of conscious experience are also the ways one is in the world. This shift of the notion of the *Lebenswelt* (lived-world) to the emphasis upon being-in-the-world expanded phenomenology in a way that allowed it to consider the totality of human relationships in the world in terms of the individual's concrete existence.

The very terminology itself, being-in-the-world, is existentialism's attempt to avoid reference to human reality in terms either of a thinking *substance* or a perceiving *subject* closed in upon itself facing physical objects which may or may not be knowable. Being-in-the-world refers exclusively to human reality in contrast to nonhuman reality, and although the specific terminology has varied among existentialists, common to all is the insistence that human reality is situated in a concrete world-context. In short, man is only man as a result of his actions which are worked out in the world. But there is still the reciprocal relationship that

---

1. Paul Ricoeur, s.v. "Phenomenologie existentielle," *Encyclopédie Française* 19 (1957):10.8–10.12. Translated in *Husserl: An Analysis of His Phenomenology*, pp. 202–12. *See* no. 52.

phenomenology insists on: The total ensemble of human actions—including thoughts, moods, efforts, emotions, and so forth—define the context in which man situates himself. But, in turn, the world-context defines and sets limits to human action.

Also central to an understanding of being-in-the-world is the existentialist insistence that this is not a concept that arises only in reflection. Even prior to reflection upon one's awareness of being-in-the-world there is already a prereflective grasp of the basic modalities which are his ways of being-in-the-world. In prereflective experience, the *subject* and *world* are not distinct; they are rather the givens of concrete experience which can only be separated by a process of abstraction. Any reflection—whether theoretical or practical—already assumes man's prereflective experience of the world and his activity in the world. The word *existence* is usually used by existentialists to refer only to human reality, for what it means to *exist* is to be always engaged in tasks in the world. Martin Heidegger even goes so far as to support this use of the term with an etymological analysis; *ex-ist* means to be outside (*ex,* "out"; *ist* "to be"). Heidegger's analysis will be discussed in more detail later.

BASIC EXISTENTIAL THEMES

It would be a mistake to view existentialist phenomenology as a single kind of philosophy, for there are many and varied kinds of existentialists. In fact, Paul Ricoeur insists that it is preferable to speak not of existentialism but of existentialisms (in the plural).[2] Although there are differences in the way various existential philosophers worked out basic themes, there are points of agreement which Ricoeur suggests can be grouped around the three following emphases: importance of the body; freedom and choice; intersubjectivity.[3]

Importance of the Body

Even a cursory reading of existentialist writings (and even the writings of Husserl) shows the importance of the body for existential phenomenology, for the body is man's basic mode of being in the world. Existentialists are here emphasizing what was implicit in Husserl[4] that

2. Paul Ricoeur, "Note sur l'existentialisme," *La Revue de l'évangélisation* 6 (1951):143.
3. Ricoeur develops these themes in his *Encyclopédie Française* article. *See* n. 1.
4. Especially in book 2 of Husserl's *Ideen,* as yet untranslated from the German. *See* no. 15.

consciousness is embodied consciousness, that is to say, consciousness incarnate. Consequently, it is incorrect, existentialists insist, to view the body as a *thing* among things and to attempt to understand it apart from its intentional structures. There is an intimate connection between consciousness and the body which is difficult to express because the soul and body dualism is so firmly ingrained in everyday modes of expression. Attempts to express this union between consciousness and body are Merleau-Ponty's term "owned-body" *(corps propre)* and Gabriel Marcel's "I am bodily." One cannot say that "I have a body" or even "I am a body," but rather "I am bodily" as incarnate subjectivity.

The existentialist emphasis upon the body provides a needed corrective to the exaggerated importance accorded to abstract reason in the philosophies of the seventeenth and eighteenth centuries. Not only did these philosophies regard reason as the human faculty par excellence, they also degraded the body to the status of another object in nature to be understood in purely mechanistic terms. Descartes, particularly, struggled with the interrelationship of reason and body; it constituted a problem that he never effectively solved. For existential phenomenology, the body is as important for an understanding of human reality as is any other dimension of existence. However, the body must be understood in terms of intentionality just as consciousness is. Moreover, the body provides the situational context for conscious experience and is the source of perspectives one has of the world. It is both the origin and organ of action in the world.

Freedom and Choice

All existentialists agree that to exist as a person is to choose freely. This emphasis follows from the phenomenological insistence that consciousness is not inserted in the causal chain, giving rise to an interpretation of freedom not only as choice but also as openness to possibilities. The present context not only provides an environment for action but also is open in terms of future possibilities. What is at issue here is the contemporary debate between those who claim that man's action is totally determined and existentialism's insistence that man is totally free. But freedom here does not mean arbitrariness but situated freedom, freedom in a context involving not only the present but also the past and the future. Freedom means self-determination in terms of open possibilities. Man does not become aware of his freedom through abstract thought or speculative argument; rather, he is aware of his freedom in the choices he makes and the actions he performs, for which he is totally responsible. It is not freedom in a negative sense as "freedom from . . ." but a positive freedom toward a multiplicity of possibilities.

Another way of emphasizing man's freedom is to insist that the unique characteristic of human reality is not only consciousness but consciousness of that consciousness or, in more traditional terms, self-consciousness. In choosing among possibilities for existence, one chooses himself. Jean-Paul Sartre makes this same point in a vivid way when he insists that the only choice one does not have is not to choose. Man is condemned to be free, as Sartre puts it.

Intersubjectivity

The third general characteristic of existential philosophy is an outgrowth of the first two. To be bodily is to exist in a world inhabited by other persons. To be with other persons is at the same time to become aware of one's freedom as well as its limitation, in that one must constantly take the other individual into account. For one discovers his own authentic humanity only by recognizing the humanity of others. Authentically existing individuals who recognize each other's humanity constitute a community. This dimension of concrete human existence cannot be ignored any more than body or freedom, for the social context in which one finds himself is also part of one's being-in-the-world. As Aristotle noted, to be alone, one must either be a beast or a god, but not a human being.[5]

Since a person shapes himself in terms of possibilities, the concrete context in which one finds himself opens up new possibilities of being human. All this is well summed up by Sartre:

> Historical situations vary; a man may be born a slave in a pagan society or a feudal lord or a proletarian. What does not vary is the necessity for him to exist in the world, to be at work there, to be there in the midst of other people, and to be mortal there. The limits are neither subjective nor objective, or, rather, they have an objective and a subjective side. Objective because they are to be found everywhere and are recognizable everywhere; subjective because they are *lived* and are nothing if man does not live them, that is, freely determine his existence with reference to them.[6]

The Humanism of Existentialism

With its emphasis on man as the center of meaning and value, existential phenomenology is echoing a humanistic ideal. In common with humanism, existentialism sees man as not only having a place in the

5. Aristotle, *Politics* 1253a. 27–30.
6. Sartre, *Existentialism*, pp. 45–46. *See* no. 204.

universe but a central place from which meaning and value radiate. In one sense, this anthropocentric view was a reaction to the collapse of the Hegelian system with its emphasis on the absolute. In light of this re-emphasis on the centrality of man, the universe is seen in terms of man's needs, projections, evaluations and so forth, and not as having a specific, determined position within the order of the totality. This shift from totality to the concrete, existing individual is a theme prominent in the nineteenth century in the writings of both Kierkegaard and Nietzsche, who provided two divergent interpretations of the humanistic ideal—theistic and atheistic. For Kierkegaard, the question of what it means to be an individual cannot be answered apart from the question of what it means to be a Christian. To be a self, for Kierkegaard, means to be grounded in the power that created it, namely, God. What this meant for Kierkegaard was that in understanding the meaning of the task of becoming an individual, one cannot ignore transcendence; transcendence (which for Kierkegaard meant God) must be included in all human values and relationships. The working out of this theme, as well as an existential analysis of the paradoxical nature of faith, constitutes a major part of Kierkegaard's work.

Nietzsche, in contrast, develops the implications of Dostoyevsky's statement that if God is dead, then all things are permitted. For Nietzsche there are no absolute or eternal values; each individual must create his own values in relation to the tasks he sets for himself. By announcing the rejection of God as the basis for values, Nietzsche also claims that man and only man decides what is valuable, meaningful, or true.

The choice between faith and unbelief, between theism and atheism, still constitutes a major area of disagreement among contemporary existentialists. Jean-Paul Sartre explicitly states this as a central point that distinguishes the major proponents of existentialism.[7] On the atheistic side are Sartre and Camus, whereas for Heidegger the question of God is still an open one. In the theistic camp are Marcel, Berdyaev, and Jaspers, although Jaspers' theism is hardly the traditional Judaeo-Christian sort which Sartre's distinction tends to imply. Sartre's distinction between theistic and atheistic existentialisms is too rigid and is likely to obscure more than it reveals. A point that should be made, which Sartre ignores, is that existential philosophy is not antithetical to religion. Indeed, existentialism is perhaps most widely known in this country through its influence on contemporary theologians, which include Tillich, Bultmann, Niebuhr, Buber, and a host of others.[8]

7. Ibid., p. 15.
8. *See* Herberg, *Four Existentialist Theologians* (no. 286) and Macquarrie, *An Existentialist Theology* (no. 288); *also see* John Macquarrie, *Twentieth-Century Religious Thought: The Frontiers of Philosophy and Theology, 1900–1960* (New York: Harper & Row, 1963).

Although existentialism is a continuation of many phenomenological themes, it has not been at the expense of a rigorous criticism of many of the basic limitations of transcendental phenomenology. Historically considered, several of the major exponents of existential phenomenology were students of Husserl who nevertheless differed with him on crucial issues arising out of the range and application of the phenomenological method. Among the better-known figures on the post-Husserlian scene are Martin Heidegger and Jean-Paul Sartre.

EXISTENTIALIST
CRITIQUE OF
TRANSCENDENTAL
PHENOMENOLOGY

Martin Heidegger

One of Husserl's preeminent students was Martin Heidegger, who not only was Husserl's assistant but was the successor to Husserl's chair at Freiburg. He was also active in the founding and editing of the *Jahrbuch für Philosophie und phänomenologische Forschung* in which he published the first part of his major work, *Being and Time (Sein und Zeit)*. This book really amounted to a major reinterpretation of phenomenology and its method. Heidegger pointed out that Husserl's attempt to describe everything as correlates of consciousness overlooked such basic dimensions of existence as dread, anxiety, forlornness, and death. In fact, according to Heidegger, even time cannot be understood as a correlate of consciousness. The method of investigating these aspects of existence cannot be that of bracketing the world (the epoche) but rather finding the basic modalities of being-in-the-world. As far back as Aristotle, Western philosophy had attempted to develop a system of categories for understanding reality. But all such systems, in Heidegger's view, treated reality—including human reality—as objects. What is needed is a new set of categories applicable to human reality as being-in-the-world.

The full development of this task as Heidegger conceived it is too complex to be discussed here, but a few summary statements about his categorial scheme will better illustrate his deviation from Husserl's eidetic phenomenology. Heidegger calls human reality *Dasein* ("being-there") in contrast to *Sein* ("Being"), which refers to Being as such. The term *Dasein* emphasizes the situatedness of human reality in the world; being there (the literal meaning of the term) stresses the fact that human existence is always existence *in* the world. *Dasein,* however, must not be understood as an entity finding itself in a world of preexisting entities, for the mode of existence of *Dasein* is not that of a thing among other things. It is rather the case that *Dasein* constitutes an openness in which entities are revealed in light of their Being. Heidegger even finds in the term *existence* itself a hint of this openness of *Dasein,* for *ex*-istence is derived from two Greek words which mean "to stand outside of." The *ex*-istence of *Dasein* (sometimes Heidegger uses the term *ecstasy*) is none other than its openness to Being in its temporal modality. The modes of being-in-the-world, however, are not conscious structures but rather constitute the world in which consciousness can function—that is, an *open* world. Whenever *Dasein* is analyzed, it becomes apparent that the ways of being-in-the-world and the way the world is are not two distinct moments of *Dasein's* existence inasmuch as *Dasein* is nothing without the world. Heidegger calls this the primordial way of existing "in truth," which is the way *Dasein* is both open to the world and the way it finds itself in the world.

Heidegger's analysis of *Dasein* is sometimes seen as an analysis of the structures of human subjectivity or, in other words, as a kind of philosophical anthropolgy. But this interpretation is mistaken inasmuch as *Dasein* is not just a structure of human reality but a structure of the world. Heidegger sees *Dasein* analysis as ontology, that is, a study of Being, for *Dasein* is the place where Being reveals itself. The way *Dasein* reveals itself is in the light of its openness toward Being, and the way Being primarily manifests itself is through what Heidegger calls the *existentialia,* or the basic modes of being-in-the-world.

The most basic mode of *Dasein* is care *(Sorge)*—care about Being, care about surrounding entities, and care about others. Care can be either authentic or inauthentic. When an individual freely chooses his way of being-in-the-world, he lives an authentic life. But when a person chooses to live on the basis of what *they* say and shapes his choices by anonymous mass opinion, he is living inauthentically. An authentic existence is characterized by: (1) finding oneself in a situation which one freely chooses; (2) understanding, which is authentic understanding of this situation; and (3) expressing this situation in authentic language. Inauthentic existence is characterized by: (1) ambiguity concerning the situation and one's relation to it; (2) lack of understanding, or mere curiosity about one's situation; and (3) expression of that curiosity in terms of facile, inauthentic speech.

These two modes of existence—authentic and inauthentic—are not given one without the other. A person finds himself in a context filled with opinions, unfounded and unwarranted claims, and the individual is compelled to live partially inauthentically. Yet his task is constantly to overcome this inauthenticity in his striving for authentic existence. The urge toward authenticity arises from the other modality of human existence, which is being-toward-death. Man is finite, and the time in which he can choose his existence is limited; thus, a person cannot postpone his choices indefinitely. Since man is finite, he is temporal and thus historical. And Heidegger's notion of historicity is one of his basic critiques of eidetic phenomenology. Husserl wanted to make a fresh beginning free from assumptions and presuppositions, but Heidegger insisted that the very language we use is historically shaped. Hence, being historical is more basic than any transcendental investigation. Here Heidegger distinguishes between two kinds of history, which he expresses by using two different German words: *Historie* and *Geschichte*. Both terms are roughly synonymous in current German usage, but Heidegger makes a distinction between them based on their etymological origins. *Historie* is the flux of events from which the individual is relatively detached and to which he is related as simply an observer or investigator. *Geschichte,* in contrast, comes from the word *geschehen,* which means "to happen," and refers in Heidegger's use to human existence in the process of happening.

Geschichte denotes existential history, namely the openness of *Dasein* toward Being in its temporal modality. In more traditional terminology, it refers to the transcendence of the present moment toward the future. When Heidegger emphasizes the temporal modality of *Dasin,* he is underscoring the fact that *Dasein* is continually outside of itself and ahead of itself. In typical fashion, Heidegger finds in the etymology of the German word for future *(Zukunft)* an acknowledgment of the transcendence of *Dasein* inasmuch as *Zukunft,* so Heidegger claims, is derived from *zu-kommen,* which means that which is "coming toward" *Dasein.* Whereas *Historie* is always in the past, *Geschichte* can only be understood in light of an openness toward both the future and the past. Failure to see this difference between *Historie* and *Geschichte,* Heidegger claims, was the major shortcoming of Husserl's eidetic reductions, for it is Heidegger's view that eidetic phenomenology was concerned mainly about *Historie,* whereas *Geschichte* is more fundamental and cannot be grasped by means of an eidetic method. This is not to imply that Heidegger accused Husserl of being entirely wrong, for Husserl's error—in Heidegger's view—was that of simply not being fundamental enough. Heidegger sees philosophy's first task as that of developing a fundamental ontology, by which he means an analysis of *Dasein.*

The development of this kind of *Dasein* analysis is the theme of *Being and Time,* which Heidegger conceived of as the first part of a larger work which would be nothing less than a critique of the entire history of Western philosophy. But as he began to work out this critique, he was led to what he considered a more fundamental problem—the question of Being itself. This change of emphasis amounts to a radical shift in Heidegger's investigations from a consideration of the question of *Dasein* to an articulation of the meaning of *Sein* ("Being"); hence, the later works of Heidegger are more concerned with *Sein* than with *Dasein*.

Heidegger points out that the question of Being, which should be the most obvious and basic question, is actually the most forgotten question simply because it is always assumed but scarcely noticed. For example, language testifies to this inasmuch as the word *being* in some form permeates all speaking. When a person says that something is, was, or will be in any particular way, he is not simply describing a thing but saying that a thing *is* in that particular way. Here the emphasis lies on *is* in order to show that there is always a difference between a thing and its Being. The problem in Western philosophy, Heidegger claimed, is that this difference is overlooked. The Western philosophical tradition has collapsed this difference by conceiving of Being as merely another being with more or less describable characteristics. The net effect is to reduce Being to the status of another thing among things. Heidegger conceives of his task as calling Western philosophy back to the question of Being, which he considers the most fundamental question in philosophy.

In his later work Heidegger has explored the possibilities of reopening the question of Being. But this effort has been less than totally successful. Heidegger himself, sensing this difficulty, observes that perhaps Being is not yet ready to reveal itself.[9] Heidegger's attempts to raise afresh the question of Being have thus far ended in the consideration that *Dasein* is the place where Being is manifested in *Geschichte*. In short, *Dasein* is the "happening" *(Das Geschehen)* where Being is revealed as time. Hence, Being can no longer be conceived of as a substance existing either in time or outside of time, as Western metaphysics since the time of Plato has viewed it. Rather, it is the case, according to Heidegger's fundamental ontology, that Being is time in the sense that Being is always coming in terms of open possibilities. Time, which is not an entity, is the open horizon in which all beings manifest themselves. Hence, Being is not a thing; but whereas it is no-thing, it is not nothingness. Being is rather the ground of all possibilities and the horizon for the interpretation of all entities.

Heidegger conceives his task as that of developing a fundamental ontology, but as has already been alluded to, fundamental ontology does not offer an explanation of things in terms of ultimate causes but is rather an explication of the meaning of Being. Since *Dasein* always finds itself as the place where Being manifests itself, fundamental ontology and analysis of *Dasein* amount to the same thing. But it must be noted that

9. Heidegger, *Holzwege* (Frankfort: Vittorio Klostermann Verlag, 1963), p. 51.

inasmuch as the meaning of Being is intimately related to time, no final announcement of the meaning of Being can be advanced. In Heidegger's view, fundamental ontology is never completed; it is always "in preparation" *(Vorbereitung)*.

Jean-Paul Sartre

Jean-Paul Sartre, the individual most closely identified with French existentialism in popular opinion, was affected by both Husserl and Heidegger, as well as by the German philosophic tradition stemming from Hegel. From Husserl Sartre gained the insight that consciousness is not a natural object or a thing. And his development of this theme constitutes some of the most rigorous analysis of the nature of consciousness to come out of the phenomenological tradition. From Heidegger Sartre accepted the notion of the situatedness, the being-there and temporalization of consciousness. And from Hegel he borrowed the dialectical structure of the relationship between consciousness and Being. These three streams—Husserlian, Heideggerian, and Hegelian—combine in Sartre's major philosophical work, *Being and Nothingness,* which deals with the nature of consciousness and the nature of Being and how these two are related. Continuing Husserl's insight that it is a mistake to analyze human reality in terms of the subject-object dichotomy, Sartre retains the noetic and noematic structures of consciousness articulated by Husserl but develops his own terminology in which to express this relationship. In place of the term *noetic* Sartre substitutes the *pour-soi* (the "for-itself") and for *noematic* he uses the term *en-soi* (the "in-itself"). In broader terms, the *pour-soi* is consciousness, the *en-soi* is Being.

The Nature of Consciousness. The for-itself *(pour-soi)* and the in-itself *(en-soi)* have a reciprocal relationship so that one is never given without the other, and neither is reducible to the other. To this extent, Sartre follows Husserl. But he goes beyond Husserl in insisting that the for-itself, since it is not an object or a thing in nature, can only be described as not-a-thing, or nothingness (literally no-thing-ness). Consciousness is therefore conceived of by Sartre as a lack or negativity which always strives to become Being or to fill itself in order to be something. Sartre has also expressed this same point in the succinct phrase, "Existence precedes essence." The essence of something refers to *what* it is; existence refers to *that* it is. For Sartre, man has no essence; he simply exists and must construct his own essence through his own free choices. Out of his own no-thing-ness, an existing individual creates his own essence and is totally responsible for it. Failure to accept this responsibility for what one is, Sartre calls "bad faith." For example, if a man defends his cowardice with reference to his high blood pressure, the state of the economy, or an unhappy childhood, it has the net effect of a refusal to accept responsibility for what he is and the situation in which he finds himself. In short, since man is self-determined, that is, determined by no-thing, he is totally responsible for what he is.

Another aspect of man's existential situation is that he always transcends the present moment by projecting himself into the future, and this determines what the past will mean. For example, an individual is faced with the future prospect of going to college. He himself determines how he will respond to this future possibility, and in so doing selects relevant aspects from his past and also changes the present with reference to this future possibility. If he claims that he cannot go to college because of his present economic situation or his past educational accomplishments, he is fleeing from his responsibility into "bad faith." This emphasis upon man's total freedom has led some to interpret Sartre as saying something merely silly, namely, that there are no limitations whatsoever on human freedom. Sartre does not mean this at all, for like Heidegger he insists upon man's situatedness. Yet he points out that any particular situation is interpreted and changed with reference to a future project, which is a freely chosen possibility. In this sense Sartre can even say that a person "chooses" his birth in the act of choosing to live rather than to commit suicide. There is always some free choice open to an individual. Free choice is the cardinal tenet of Sartre's existential philosophy. The only choice man does not have is the choice of not choosing.

Being-in-Itself. Sartre refers to nonhuman reality as being in-itself. The only way he can describe the in-itself is in terms of such metaphors as opaque, dense, absurd. Anything else that can be said of the in-itself is in terms of the projects of the for-itself, or what Husserl called the "intentionality of consciousness." Thus, for Sartre, consciousness is constantly directed toward Being but it continuously transcends Being by introducing future possibilities. And since the future dimension of temporality is the not-yet, the for-itself is constantly introducing negativity into the in-itself in continued transcendence toward the future. Here is one of the fundamental points of disagreement between Sartre and Heidegger: Heidegger's negativity was only in terms of death, or the "nothingness which makes naught" *(das Nichts selbst nichtet)* as Heidegger puts it. For Sartre, negativity is involved in every judgment, the negative not only of the future (the "not yet") but also of the past (the "no longer"). It is this constant dialectic between Being and nothingness that, for Sartre, constitutes the basic structure of consciousness. But consciousness never completely fulfills itself; it is constantly transcending itself in ever new projects in such a way that it can never see itself as a fixed entity. At any given time it can only see what it has made of itself in the past in terms of an open future filled with not-yet-realized possibilities. This view of the ego, or self, constitutes a major difference between Sartre and Husserl. For Husserl, the ego is transcendental and can never be bracketed; for Sartre the ego is not identical with consciousness. The ego is rather what consciousness has made of itself in the past. To express this rather paradoxical notion of the self, Sartre suggests the metaphor of the ego as the trail of concretized possibilities (the sum total of past choices) that consciousness leaves behind it. This allows Sartre to make the paradoxical statement: "The nature of consciousness is to be what it is not and not to be what it is."[10]

Like Heidegger, Sartre has shifted his emphasis in his later writings, although it is a matter of continued debate whether this shift amounts to a radical change in his view or a refinement of his earlier position. Although Sartre continues to insist that man is totally free, this freedom is always historically situated. Thus, for Sartre, any philosophy is also historically situated in a widely varied social, political, and economic context. And since the conditions that gave rise to Marxism have not changed, Sartre sees Marxism as the basic philosophy of contemporary times. Of course, Sartre disagrees with the deterministic interpretation of man as suggested by dialectical materialism, which sees man as only a product of social and economic conditions. But Sartre is in agreement with the basic Marxist contention that man realizes himself only in action. This follows from Sartre's commitment to the intentional structure of consciousness as always directed outward toward the world. And it is in the world that man, through his own freely chosen actions, works out the implications of his choices. By introducing the notion of absolute freedom into Marxism, Sartre feels he has purified it and pointed it toward a concrete and open direction. Consequently, Sartre is currently the severest critic and the most ardent advocate of Marxist socialism. This stance has shifted interest from his philosophical works to his political activism, which frequently has involved him in highly debatable causes. It is probably in his dramatic works, written for the theater, that his influence has been most widely felt.

EXISTENTIALISM AS A
LITERARY MOVEMENT

Early in his career, Sartre publicly stated that existentialism was not a popular kind of philosophy but was rather a philosophy for the specialist, a statement that is probably the most disregarded comment ever made by an existentialist.[11] In his late work Sartre, in opposition to this

10. Sartre, *Being and Nothingness*, p. 70. *See* no. 199.
11. Sartre, *Existentialism*, p. 15. *See* no. 204.

previous position, claimed that existentialism is not philosophical thought but must be surpassed by critical Marxism.[12] This changed attitude reflects a tension that has always been present in existentialism, namely the tension between systematic and nonsystematic philosophy. The nonsystematic stance (one could almost say antisystematic attitude) is found in the writings of both Kierkegaard and Nietzsche. But with the introduction of the phenomenological method into the tradition, an increasing amount of systematization was called for, and has been expressed in varied genre. Existentialist writers have turned to drama, novels, short stories, poetry, as well as the essay form in order to communicate their understanding of the nature of human reality in concrete situations. This indirect method of communication is quite consistent with the existentialist view that one cannot coerce another's freedom; yet at the same time these varied modes of writing enable them to reveal the universal human predicament. Every particular situation suggests a possibility that could be lived by any human being.

As a result of the choice of literary genre by several prominent existential thinkers (notably Sartre), existentialism first gained attention in the United States as a literary movement. After the Second World War, attention was focused on the plays of Sartre and the novels and short stories of Albert Camus. Consequently, increased concern was directed to the precursors of existentialism, Gide, Rilke, and Baudelaire. From these diverse streams arose the literature and theater of the absurd and the rereading of the works of Kafka, Dostoyevsky, and the contemporary writer Samuel Beckett. All these, as well as a host of others, have loosely been classified as existential writers, but the only real points of contact consist of the commonality of basic themes—alienation, rebellion, absurdity, despair, forlornness, and so forth. The same kind of influence of existentialism so prominent in western Europe and the United States had a comparable effect in eastern Europe. Such writers as Kolakowski, Schaff, and Petrović, while standing up against existentialism, had to face the same themes which they introduced into the context of Marxist thought.

To be completely accurate, however, one would be well advised to limit the use of the term *existentialist* to those writers whose dramatic and literary works echo a consciously articulated philosophical view. Sartre, of course, is the most obvious example. In Europe Gabriel Marcel is known as widely as a playwright as he is a philosopher, although his dramatic works have gained little notoriety in this country and have not been translated into English. Even Camus, who is generally regarded as an existentialist writer, did not consider himself to be an existentialist.

12. Sartre, *Critique de la raison dialectique*, p. 17. *See* no. 413.

And had he not suffered a premature death, he would have probably moved away from the absurdist theme, a movement already apparent in one of his later novels *The Plague*. But because of the influence existentialist philosophy has had on literature, many persons first became acquainted with existential themes in their literary expression.

OTHER PROMINENT EXISTENTIALISTS

No discussion of the influence of existential philosophy would be complete without some reference to other leading thinkers, with some mention of their varied national backgrounds—which points up the fact that existentialism is not a philosophical movement restricted to a single country or even a single continent. No summary statement can do justice to the varied richness and profundity of the work of these thinkers, but reference to their work here is centered on those themes not articulated by other thinkers in the existentialist tradition.

Nicholas Berdyaev

Nicholas Berdyaev (sometimes spelled Nikolai Berdiaeff, or a similar variation), having lived through the enslavement of man by a Marxist-Leninist system in which he played a prominent role, developed an existentialist philosophy emphasizing spiritual freedom. The aspect of human reality most endangered by contemporary philosophical and political movements, according to Berdyaev, is the human spirit. In his work he offers an exhaustive analysis of those aspects of life that threaten to enslave man's spirit—the state, society, culture, history, revolution, possessions, and all forms of dogmatism. In opposition to all forms of authoritarianism, Berdyaev emphasizes the priority of the person; hence, he refers to his view as "personalism" (not to be confused, however, with the use of this term by Emmnauel Mounier). Berdyaev stresses that antithetical to authority is personal *authorship* which is creative rather than dogmatic. He further claims that any authoritarian system is forced to use power because it has lost its authorship to solve problems. *Authorship* means the exchange of ideas, free and open discussion, and mutual respect. And since dogmatic thinking by its very nature is not free, creative persons are inevitably suppressed or destroyed by such systems. But, for Berdyaev, freedom is not easily given but is rather the major task of spirit. It is always easier to submit and succumb to authority rather than to face up to the difficult task of becoming free.

It would be a mistake, however, to understand Berdyaev's reference to authority as referring only to an externally imposed system. Authority, as he sees it, is any enslaving factor which threatens human freedom. Perhaps the most vicious forms of enslavement are those imposed by the individual himself, such as the will to rule, will to possess, will to dominate. Reflecting a Hegelian view, Berdyaev points out that masters and slaves are really in the same boat; they are both victims of slavery. For to be a person, one must define himself only in terms of his own spiritual freedom, not with reference to possessions, structures of authority, passions, or by domination of others. Here Berdyaev is in agreement with the basic existentialist emphasis on freedom, so that the enslavement of one man is the enslavement of all. Because he lived through and participated in the Russian Communist revolution, Berdyaev has a unique perspective from which to assess the dehumanizing aspects of contemporary political systems. Berdyaev's works consist of a massive critique of all aspects of the twentieth-century world and show the applicability of existentialist themes to a broad range of human situations.

Gabriel Marcel

The work of Gabriel Marcel, while in continuity with general existentialist themes, points to a factor in experience not usually developed by other writers in the tradition. From its very origins, existential philosophy has expressed a distrust of elaborate rational systems which purport to supply a total and comprehensive view of man in the world. Marcel also rejects such systems and points to the irreducible opacity and the profound depth of human existence which, he claims, can never be fully understood by any objective method.

To show why this is the case, Marcel makes a fundamental distinction between *being* and *having*. What a person has, to a certain extent, is external to him; *having* pertains to the objective order of things, and one can exercise a certain amount of control (by means of an appropriate technique) over the objective order of reality. But having, as Marcel describes it, is subordinate to one's being, and the tension between being and having (a tension that is unavoidable) is seen vividly in reflection on one's own body. The body is both something that I am and something that I have. My body is the basic condition for any act of having, inasmuch as control over one's own body is the sine qua non of any possible relationship with the world of objects. One's body, however, presents itself as more than an object—as more than something I *have*—for it is the mode of one's being in the world. To be a human being is to *be bodily*.

Reflection on one's incarnate, or bodily, mode of being in the world further highlights the depth of human existence, which Marcel emphasizes by the distinction between *problem* and *mystery*. A *problem* is an inquiry from which the inquirer is detached, for which he can find appropriate methods of investigation, and to which he can propose tentative solutions. If he does not have a solution to the problem, it can be accounted for as a function of the lack of data or due to an improper technique of analysis. But not all human concerns are problems. To so treat them is to overlook the importance of mystery. A *mystery,* in contrast to a problem, is that in which the observer participates and from which he can never extricate himself. Life must be seen as mystery and not problem, Marcel insists, for one can never extricate himself from life and view it from a completely objective manner or with a thoroughly detached viewpoint.

Correlated with having is the problematic and the resulting modes of thought appropriate to problems, such as curiosity and, in a more systematic way, the scientific modes of inquiry. Mystery, however, is closed to scientific analysis, and the appropriate response to mystery is wonder, which leads to wisdom. The upshot of Marcel's analysis is that all efforts to systematize life are doomed to failure, for such attempts ignore the irreducible depth of the mystery of existence.

Also considered as mysteries by Marcel are evil, love, embodiment, and Being itself. The constant temptation is to reduce mysteries to problems, but this results in a degradation and falsification of human life. One can never exhaustively analyze a mystery; this much is certain for Marcel. But this state of things need not lead to despair, for it is a central element in Marcel's thought that man, in his freedom, can respond to mystery in a movement that can best be described as hope. But by *hope,* Marcel does not mean simple optimism or stoic acceptance. He sees hope not as directed toward any particular thing but rather as a response to Being itself. Hope is bound up in the mystery of Being so that it, too, always remains beyond complete rational comprehension. And hope cannot be justified by anything other than itself.

Marcel's insistence on the mystery of Being points up the irreducibility of human existence to a merely spatio-temporal reality. For man to view himself as only a physical object is to degrade and falsify himself and to fall into what Marcel calls a "tragic error." Marcel sees man as a self-transcending reality; man is both a thing and yet more than a thing. And this too is a mystery. Whenever one evaluates his actions or judges the present moment, he is going beyond himself in a movement of self-transcendence which is not explainable in terms of the given situation. Man's relation to Being as mystery, although not capable of discursive or rational explanation, is glimpsed in certain intensely lived situations, the most important of which for Marcel are faith, hope, and love. Reflection on these experiences points to the fundamental mystery itself—the mystery of Being.

Karl Jaspers

The priority of Being for philosophical reflection, which one sees in Marcel's work, is echoed in the thought of Karl Jaspers. Originally trained as a psychiatrist, and having written widely in the field of psychiatry, Jaspers came to realize the limitations of this science and its inability to deal with the basic aspects of human existence. His subsequent philosophical work has made significant contributions to the application of existential insights to psychology, but discussion here will focus on his properly philosophical work and will emphasize themes unique to Jaspers' thought not discussed by other existentialists.

Like Marcel, Jaspers finds the question of Being to be the all-important question, but unlike Marcel he does not work out this theme within the context of specifically Christian thought. In agreement with other existentialists, notably Heidegger, Jaspers argues that it is a mistake to identify Being with the sum total of things. Being is neither the name for the class comprising all entities, nor is it the highest entity among entities. In other words, if one were cataloging all reality, he would not place Being at the top of the list with all lesser entities subsumed under it. The existentialist claim is that the traditional notion of Being as a specific, describable, definable entity is incorrect and misguided. Being is not definable by any objective characteristics; it is not even open to direct philosophical reflection but is approachable only indirectly from various limited perspectives. Being is neither objective nor subjective. It is beyond all such classifications, yet it encompasses both. Jaspers attempts to capture this sense of Being by referring to it as the "Encompassing" (Umgreifende). The Encompassing is that from which all objective and subjective knowledge draws its meaning and its limits.

The Encompassing is one of the most difficult concepts in Jaspers' philosophy—difficult for the reason that it is beyond the subject-object dichotomy and can therefore only be approached by indirect means. The Encompassing embraces all distinctions, but it can be grasped indirectly in its various modes. Jaspers discusses several of these modes, but usually they are subsumed under two: The Encompassing That We Are, and The Encompassing That Is Being Itself. This distinction can be recognized as akin to the distinction between subject and object, self and world; but what is novel in Jaspers' approach is that there is no ultimate distinction between subject and object inasmuch as both are rooted in the Encompassing itself. The Encompassing That We Are (loosely called subjectivity) and The Encompassing That Is Being Itself (objectivity in Jaspers' refined sense) can be further analyzed into the additional modes of the Encompassing which are perhaps more easily grasped in figure 1.

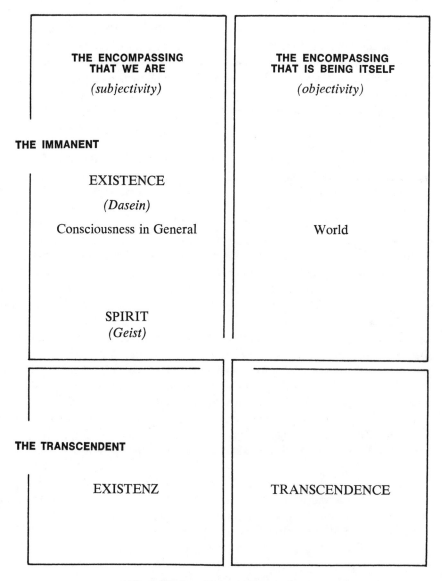

Fig. 1. Modes of Jaspers' Encompassing

The self is approachable in a number of ways, the most primitive of which is *Dasein*. As *Dasein,* one is aware of one's needs, desires, everyday concerns about things, and concern about the surrounding nature that fulfills these needs. It is important to note that Jaspers uses the term *Dasein* in a completely different sense than Heidegger does. Whereas for Heidegger *Dasein* is an ontological opening to Being, for Jaspers *Dasein* signifies only the ordinary, everyday levels of consciousness. *Dasein* or "existence," as it is sometimes translated, refers to a sentient being in a state of nature, relating to the natural environment and concerned to preserve his own continuity. At the level of *Dasein* one is not concerned with moral, religious, or esthetic values; right and wrong, justice and injustice, have no place. Hedonism and power are the basic relationships. Knowledge is only an instrument, and truth has only a utilitarian value.

A higher level of consciousness is what Jaspers calls consciousness in general, which consists of scientific and categorial knowledge. As consciousness in general, man searches for the understanding of objective reality and all its laws. Through understanding, man relates to the world in terms of such intangible objects as genus and species, scientific principles, and esthetic as well as ethical norms. Logic and objective relations with nature in terms of what Kant would call "judgments" arise at this level. In short, truth is both factual and logical.

But when one asks more fundamental questions, he discovers that answers to them cannot be given through a course of logical arguments or measured by a standard of deductive correctness. At the level of consciousness in general, one cannot make sense of romantic love, understand literature, appreciate art, or have metaphysics and religion. They all require a mode of understanding which is spiritual. As spirit, man shapes an idea which presents a unified view of the world and his relation to it. The life of spirit gives birth to ideas which furnish the background for human thoughts and actions, and these ideas are manifested in all human endeavors. Such ideas as those of soul, God, world, social order, justice, virtue, and beauty are not only theoretical but are guides in life. Following Kant, Jaspers suggests that these ideas do not constitute objective knowledge but provide a context which makes the world intelligible to rational beings.

These modes of the Encompassing—*Dasein,* consciousness in general, and spirit—are found in the world in an immanent way. Jaspers insists, however, that all these modes are found to be lacking. Even at the level of spirit man finds himself in a context of general ideas, norms, and values which do not deal with his uniqueness. The unique particularity of each individual can only be grasped by him in a movement toward transcendence, which Jaspers calls *Existenz*. *Existenz* is a difficult notion to understand, but it can be pointed to in a number of ways. As *Existenz,* man is open to his unlimited potentiality, which encompasses the developing spirit and consciousness in general, but which at the same time is related to transcendence. *Existenz* is always a self-transcending movement which can be glimpsed in all philosophizing and in authentically free decisions. The level of *Existenz,* however, can only be attained in freedom and by a break with all inauthentic modes of existence that Jaspers characterizes as a "leap." *Existenz* is a refusal to objectify and dehumanize human reality and is an affirmation of man's free and creative relationship with transcendence.

All this is Jaspers' way of insisting that the Encompassing can only be approached in the disclosures of it that are present in and through man. Man's self-transcending movement is always directed toward the world, but it always falls short and points toward that which transcends the world, namely Being itself. Although Jaspers sometimes uses the word God to refer to Being, he cannot be interpreted as referring to the God of traditional theism who can be reached by formal proofs or objective reasoning. For Jaspers, the way toward Being is through what he calls "cipher" reading. What can be objectively thought is rejected as inadequate and inapplicable to transcendence. Being cannot be defined by a series of predicates, or by inferences—although Jaspers suggests a kind of via negativa when he says that all categories of thought can be employed by saying that they are what Being is not; that is, they do not apply to Being. All this is similar to reading the "signs" of *Existenz*— freedom, resolution, perseverance—which do not define *Existenz* but point to it.

Existenz gains access to transcendence by such ciphers as religious images, representations, and beliefs which have a meaning but do not mean any specific object. The ciphers, of course, depend upon the historical situation of *Existenz* in how they signify and point to transcendence. Jaspers further claims that man's awareness of Being arises in "limit situations" such as death, suffering, struggle, chance, guilt, and faith. These ultimate situations cannot be overcome or changed; they can only be acknowledged. Yet they reveal man's being to himself in a partial way by pointing to the presence of "gaps" in the world and the failure of all efforts to understand the world in terms of itself. These "limit situations," however, cannot be forced or proved; they are rather the fulfilled historicity of man's *Existenz.*

Jaspers' approach to Being through the concrete situation of man shows his interest in factual description as well as its limitations. It also points up his previous training as a psychiatrist and his realization that purely scientific description cannot do justice to the basic dimensions of human existence. Because of the centrality of the Encompassing in Jaspers' philosophy, he has been compared to Eastern mysticism, but this is not an adequate comparison. Jaspers is led to the notion of the Encompassing because of what he considers to be the basic aspect of human experience, man's self-transcending movement in a search for totality. A better comparison would be with the pre-Socratic Greek tradition and its emphasis on understanding man's specificity in the context of totality and man's desire for knowledge of true Being. But Jaspers is through and through an existentialist due to his insistence that the question of Being itself cannot be separated from man's concrete situation. "That is why," Jaspers notes, "all philosophical discourse is so incomplete. It calls for completion out of the being of him who hears it. Philosophy does not give, it can only awaken—it can remind, and help to secure and preserve."[13]

BIBLIOGRAPHY

The following bibliography concentrates on general studies of existential philosophy featuring discussions of common themes in central figures. For more extensive bibliographies of individual philosophers, see the appendix which contains listings of primary sources and critical studies on Heidegger, Sartre, Berdyaev, Marcel, and Jaspers, as well as other thinkers in the phenomenological-existential tradition such as Maurice Merleau-Ponty and Paul Ricoeur.

General Studies in Existentialism

150. Abbagnano, Nicola. *Critical Existentialism*. Translated by Nino Langiulli. Garden City, N.Y.: Doubleday, Anchor Books, 1967.
    General discussion of existentialism's response to traditional philosophic questions.

151. Allen, E. L. *Existentialism from Within*. New York: Macmillan, 1953.
    Deals with the concepts of reason, history, faith, and mystery in existentialist thought.

152. Barnes, Hazel Estella. *An Existentialist Ethics*. New York: Knopf, 1967.
    Discusses basic questions of freedom and choice and treats the differing existential positions from a humanistic viewpoint.

153. Barrett, William. *Irrational Man: A Study in Existential Philosophy*. Garden City, N.Y.: Doubleday, Anchor, 1958.
    Discussion of existentialism as expressing the spirit of contemporary

13. Jaspers, *Way to Wisdom*, p. 51. *See* no. 371.

times with particular attention to the thought of Kierkegaard, Nietzsche, Heidegger, and Sartre.

154. ———. *What Is Existentialism?* New York: Grove, 1964.
Analysis of general existentialist themes with a detailed treatment of Heidegger showing his later drift away from existential philosophy.

155. Blackham, H. J. *Six Existentialist Thinkers.* New York: Harper & Row, Harper Torchbooks, 1959.
Analysis of the thought of Kierkegaard, Nietzsche, Marcel, Jaspers, Heidegger, and Sartre; extensive bibliography.

156. Boelen, Bernard J. *Existential Thinking.* Pittsburgh: Duquesne Univ. Pr., 1968.
Approaches existentialism from the perspective of traditional philosophical wonder; deals with ethics, esthetics, and transcendence.

157. Collins, James. *The Existentialists.* Chicago: Regnery, Gateway, 1952.
Existential backgrounds in Kierkegaard, Nietzsche, and Husserl with an analysis of contemporary existentialists such as Sartre, Jaspers, Marcel, and Heidegger; extensive bibliography.

158. Douglas, Kenneth. *A Critical Bibliography of Existentialism.* New York: Kraus Reprint, 1966.
Reprint of Special Monograph No. 4 from *Yale French Studies* listing books and articles by and about Sartre, Simone de Beauvoir, and Merleau-Ponty.

159. Grene, Marjorie. *Introduction to Existentialism.* Chicago: Univ. of Chicago Pr., 1959.
Originally published under the title *Dreadful Freedom;* contains discussion of Kierkegaard, Heidegger, Sartre, Jaspers, and Marcel.

160. Grimsley, Ronald. *Existentialist Thought.* Mystic, Conn.: Verry, Lawrence, 1955.
Outline of the basic themes in Kierkegaard, Heidegger, Jaspers, Sartre, and Marcel.

161. Harper, Ralph. *Existentialism: A Theory of Man.* Cambridge, Mass.: Harvard Univ. Pr., 1948.

162. Heinemann, F. H. *Existentialism and the Modern Predicament.* New York: Harper & Row, Harper Torchbooks, 1958.
Analysis of origins and development of existential philosophy with reference to the thought of Husserl, Heidegger, Sartre, Marcel, Jaspers, and Berdyaev.

163. Kaufmann, Walter, ed. *Existentialism from Dostoevsky to Sartre*. New York: Meridian, 1956.
Excerpts and original translations from the works of Dostoevsky, Kierkegaard, Nietzsche, and Sartre.

164. Knight, Everett W. *Literature Considered as Philosophy: The French Example*. New York: Macmillan, 1962.
Shows how existential themes have been expressed in the literary works of Sartre, Camus, and Simone de Beauvoir.

165. Langiulli, Nino, ed. *Existentialist Tradition*. Garden City, N.Y.: Doubleday, 1971.
Representative selections from existentialist philosophers.

166. Lawrence, Nathaniel, and O'Connor, Daniel, eds. *Readings in Existential Phenomenology*. Englewood Cliffs, N.J.: Prentice-Hall, 1967.
Articles and excerpts dealing with the phenomenological-existential treatment of consciousness, embodiment, values, and existential perspectives in psychology, sociology, and anthropology.

167. Lee, Edward L., and Mandelbaum, Maurice, eds. *Phenomenology and Existentialism*. Baltimore: Johns Hopkins Pr., 1967.
Articles by leading philosophers dealing with a variety of themes and specific problems in the thought of Husserl, Sartre, Merleau-Ponty, and Heidegger.

168. Luijpen, William A. *Existential Phenomenology*. Pittsburgh: Duquesne Univ. Pr., 1960.
Discussion of traditional problems leading to phenomenology; specific attention to the nature of man, freedom, truth, and metaphysics.

169. ———. *Phenomenology and Humanism: A Primer in Existential Phenomenology*. Pittsburgh: Duquesne Univ. Pr., 1966.

170. ———, and Koren, Henry J. *A First Introduction to Existential Phenomenology*. Pittsburgh: Duquesne Univ. Pr., 1969.
Focuses on major existential themes and thinkers; bibliography of significant figures in existentialism.

171. Mounier, Emmanuel. *Existentialist Philosophies: An Introduction*. New York: Macmillan, 1949.
Analysis of major themes of existentialism from the viewpoint of a leading French thinker and founder of the movement known as personalism.

172. Naumann, Elmo. *New Dictionary of Existentialism*. New York: Philosophical Library, 1971.

173. Olson, Robert G. *Introduction to Existentialism.* New York: Dover, 1962.
Shows the relationship of Sartre and Heidegger to the philosophical
tradition and clarifies the existentialist attitude toward the human condition.

174. Reinhardt, Kurt F. *Existentialist Revolt.* 2d ed. New York: Frederick,
n.d.
Deals topically with different existentialists and focuses on such themes
as God, man, truth, Being, and the basic structure of existentialism.

175. Sadler, William A., Jr. *Existence and Love: A New Approach in Existen-
tial Phenomenology.* New York: Scribner, n.d.
Deals with the concept of love and introduces the works of Scheler and
Binswanger unavailable in English.

176. Sanborn, Patricia F. *Existentialism.* New York: Pegasus, 1968.
General discussion of common existential themes focusing on the
thought of Kierkegaard, Jaspers, Marcel, Sartre, and Heidegger.

177. Schrader, G. A., ed. *Existential Philosophers: Kierkegaard to Merleau-
Ponty.* New York: McGraw-Hill, 1967.
Excerpts from major existential philosophers.

178. Ussher, Arland. *Journey through Dread.* New York: Biblo & Tannen,
1955.
Discussion of Kierkegaard's concept of encounter with God, Heidegger's concept of encounter with death, and Sartre's notion of encounter of
the other.

179. Wahl, Jean. *Philosophies of Existence: An Introduction to the Basic
Thoughts of Kierkegaard, Heidegger, Jaspers, Marcel, Sartre.* New York:
Schocken, 1969.

180. ———. *A Short History of Existentialism.* Translated by Forrest Williams
and Stanley Maron. New York: Philosophical Library, 1949.
Shows roots of existentialism in Kierkegaard and briefly treats Jaspers,
Heidegger, and Sartre; includes transcript of a discussion of existentialism
by Nicholas Berdyaev, Maurice de Gandillac, Georges Gurvitch, Alexandre Koyré, Emmanuel Levinas, and Gabriel Marcel.

181. Warnock, Mary. *Existentialism.* London: Oxford Univ. Pr., 1970.
Major themes in Nietzsche, Husserl, Heidegger, Merleau-Ponty, and
Sartre.

182. ———. *Existentialist Ethics.* New York: St. Martins, 1967.
   Analysis of the ethical theories implicit in the thought of Kirkegaard, Heidegger, and Sartre.

183. Wild, John. *The Challenge of Existentialism.* Bloomington, Ind.: Indiana Univ. Pr., 1955.
   Comprehensive discussion of the origins of existential philosophy and its major themes with reference to the full range of philosophical questions; extensive bibliography.

184. ———. *Existence and the World of Freedom.* Englewood Cliffs, N.J.: Prentice-Hall, 1963.
   Discussion of the problem of freedom in traditional philosophies with specific attention to the phenomenological notion of lived-world in which freedom and responsibility function.

185. Wilson, Colin. *Introduction to the New Existentialism.* Boston: Houghton Mifflin, 1967.

186. Winn, Ralph B., comp. *A Concise Dictionary of Existentialism.* New York: Philosophical Library, 1960.
   Not a dictionary but a collection of quotations from various existential philosophers arranged alphabetically under widely varied headings.

   Also see nos. 45, 52, 53, 73, 85, 86, 110, 111, 113, 118.

Marxism and Existentialism

The relation between Marxism and existentialism is a theme increasingly explored, especially in France, due in part to Sartre's political activism. The following selected listing provides a general treatment of this interaction; for more specific studies, see the bibliographies on Sartre and Merleau-Ponty in the appendix.

187. Aron, Raymond. *Marxism and the Existentialists.* New York: Harper & Row, 1969.
   Written by a leading French thinker, this study focuses especially on the Marxism of Sartre.

188. Blakely, Thomas J. "Current Soviet Views on Existentialism." *Studies in Soviet Thought* 7 (1967):333–39.
   Discussion of the official Soviet attitude toward existentialism as merely a subjective reaction of no philosophic value.

189. Lessing, Arthur. "Marxist Existentialism." *Review of Metaphysics* 20 (1970):461–84.
   Good discussion of the literature with particular attention to Sartre.

190. Odajnyk, Walter. *Marxism and Existentialism*. Garden City, N.Y.: Doubleday, Anchor, 1965.
   Shows how the phenomenological notion of intentionality makes possible a rapproachement with the Marxist emphasis on praxis.

191. Schaff, Adam. *Philosophy of Man*. New York: Dell, 1968.
   Collection of essays countering the influence of existentialism in Eastern Europe in terms of Marxist humanism.

CHAPTER 5

TRADITIONAL PROBLEMS PHENOMENOLOGICALLY TREATED

The discussion in previous chapters has shown that phenomenology is not a new set of doctrines but a way of renewing traditional problems that have dominated Western philosophy since its inception among the Greeks. In this sense, phenomenologists do not consider themselves as doing anything new or strange. But in the context of modern philosophy (i.e., philosophy since the time of Descartes) the traditional philosophical questions have been downgraded—or even eliminated entirely—by being reduced to questions more appropriate to the particular natural sciences such as biology, chemistry, physics, and so forth. Such questions as the nature of the self, freedom, experience, values, and human relationships, according to phenomenology, remain nevertheless the perennial concerns of philosophy and cannot be relegated to particular sciences. This is not to say that science cannot shed light on these questions; indeed it can and must. But the fatal error in much contemporary philosophy is the assumption that science, and science alone, can give the fundamental responses to these particularly human concerns. A case in point is the philosophy of mind. A popular and pervasive explanation of mind is that mental activity can be totally accounted for in terms of physical processes which are the proper domain of psychophysiology. In turn, this kind of explanation further reduces its principles of understanding to those natural laws investigated by chemistry and, ultimately, physics.

This kind of response to traditional philosophical problems signals a radical reductionism which phenomenologists often refer to as "nothing but" philosophy: mental activity is "nothing but" physical processes in the brain; freedom is "nothing but" an illusion due to a lack of proper knowledge of causal relationships; values are "nothing but" emotional preferences explainable in terms of chemical imbalance; perception is "nothing but" the physical interaction of different states of matter. The basic assumption underlying all such explanations is that reality is "nothing but" the sum total of physical entities. Phenomenology's response is to insist that all such assumptions be bracketed (the phenomenological epoche). By suspending these presuppositions, the phenomenologist does not thereby conclude that such explanations are incorrect but that they must be set aside, put in parentheses as it were, until they can be philosophically validated. In short, phenomenology insists that phenomena be investigated as they present themselves to consciousness; then and only then can they be placed in the proper perspective, taking care that no area of conscious experience be excluded or reduced to something other than what is being experienced. Before one can conclude that mental activity is "nothing but" physical processes in the brain, he must already know the mental activity as it is in itself. But the only way one can know mental activity as it is in itself is by examining it as phenomenon, that is as it appears in conscious experience. The phenomenological method offers a way of doing this.

CONSCIOUSNESS
AND THE SELF

Since Descartes the concept of the self has been one of the predominant themes in philosophy. Descartes' conclusions have been seen to be inadequate, but the primacy of the question of the self is as important as ever. This question is crucial for phenomenology inasmuch as consciousness is the point of departure for any philosophizing. Discussion in previous chapters has shown that a central aspect of the phenomeonological method is the intentional structure of consciousness. There is no need to repeat that discussion here; the reader is rather referred to the relevant sections of chapters 1 and 2. But to pinpoint what the intentionality of consciousness implies for the concept of the self, one or two summary statements will be helpful.

The phenomenon of consciousness, when investigated phenomenologically, reveals its intentionality; that is, consciousness is never experienced as a *thing,* an entity among entities, but rather as an activity. This activity, however, is never closed in upon itself or empty; it is always directed beyond itself towards something other than itself. One can speak of the *objects* of consciousness as that towards which consciousness is directed, but it is important not to understand *object* to mean only a physical object (a temptation resulting from the scientific prejudices of our age). Physical objects may indeed be an intentional object of consciousness, but so may nonphysical objects: theories, numbers, values, other selves, future possibilities, emotions, moods, and so forth. Failure to understand the full range of possible experience results in a considerable narrowing of philosophical investigation. To repeat another word of caution, it is important not to confuse *intentionality* as a philosophic notion with the ordinary language use of the term. One can speak of intending to do something, meaning by that a deliberate action on his part. This is certainly one case of the intentionality of consciousness in the philosophical sense, but when phenomenology speaks of *intentionality,* it includes all conscious orientations.

When one views consciousness as phenomenon (i.e., freed from all presuppositions about the nature of consciousness) one discovers its intentional structure. But more than that, one also discovers that not everything can be bracketed, for the process of bracketing itself can only be accomplished by a self which can never be bracketed. Husserl referred to it as the phenomenological "residue" and labeled it the "transcendental ego." Husserl argued that the ego and its conscious life could also be investigated directly by the phenomenological method, but this claim was a controversial one challenged by Sartre, Heidegger, and Merleau-Ponty. Husserl's notion of the transcendental ego and its investigation by means of eidetic phenomenology has already been briefly discussed in chapter 3 *(see* pp. 38–39).[1] Rather than expand on Husserl's notion of transcendental ego, this discussion will focus on post-Husserlian treatment of the self and its inseparable relation to consciousness. Most of the recent phenomenological studies of the self have avoided Husserl's transcendental method in favor of a more concrete analysis of the self in its relation to the world.

When consciousness is investigated phenomenologically, its intentional structure reveals that the self, or ego, is always implicit in any conscious activity. Whatever their differences, all phenomenologists would agree that the self *(ego)* cannot be separated from its conscious activity *(cognito)* which is always directed toward some object *(cogitatum).* This active process, *ego-cogito-cogitatum,* is always presented as a unity, but investi-

1. For Husserl's analysis of the ego, *see* nos. 12, 15.

gation can be centered on one of its poles, with the proviso that neither pole of this unity can be understood in isolation from the other. But at this point disagreements arise among phenomenologists, for how does one become aware of the ego? Two principal views have been offered: (1) the ego is so implicit in all consciousness that it can never be grasped as it is in itself; or (2) the ego can become an object of consciousness and can be investigated just as any other object. The former view was held by Merleau-Ponty, who claimed that the self is immanent in all conscious life and any attempt to investigate consciousness apart from the self is doomed to failure. The latter view is held by Sartre, who insists that the ego is a product of conscious activity but is not identical with it. For Sartre, the ego is the total of all past conscious activity and becomes known when consciousness reflects upon this past activity. In this sense one can say that, for Sartre, consciousness is nonegological, and he distinguishes between the self or ego, and consciousness.

Subsequent investigation into the nature of the self has shown that these two responses are not total explanations; both are partial and limited perspectives. The work of Paul Ricoeur has demonstrated that both the views just discussed can be incorporated into a larger explanation which shows that every aspect of conscious life is a partial manifestation of the self. Ricoeur has pointed out that the intentional structure of consciousness must be extended to include actions as well as thoughts. Actions, like consciousness, are always directed toward something, and in any action one becomes aware of the self as author of the act.[2] On the one hand, the self is not given to consciousness inasmuch as it is never separate from a matrix of actions. In this sense, Merleau-Ponty was right. But on the other hand, the self is one pole of this matrix of acts, namely the author of them. Through these acts one can trace out the intentions of the self, and the self in this sense becomes an object of investigation. One can therefore say that Sartre was also right. The upshot of Ricoeur's analysis is that the self is never totally knowable but it is always partially knowable in its specific acts.

In line with the above discussion, most phenomenologists make a distinction between *reflective* and *prereflective* consciousness. *Reflective* consciousness (that is, self-consciousness) arises in the way that has just been detailed, namely, as awareness of the self, as author and originator of actions, in relation to the world. Most phenomenologists, however, argue that there is also a *prereflective* awareness of the world, which is an activity of consciousness unaware of itself. Reflective consciousness, in contrast, is awareness of the activity performed by prereflective consciousness. An example will clarify the meaning of this distinction. In

2. Ricoeur, *Freedom and Nature,* pp. 56ff. *See* no. 203.

counting, one is not first aware of the activity of counting but rather of the objects being counted. But if one should make a mistake while counting, this forces attention to the activity of counting itself. Or one could simply shift his attention from the objects being counted to the activity of counting in order to understand better the nature of this activity. This shift, however, signals a change from the prereflective (the act of counting) to the reflective (awareness of the act of counting). In actual conscious life these shifts occur constantly without any need for deliberate refocusing of attention, which points up the fact that even in prereflective consciousness the self is involved as an intending subject directing conscious activity.

This view of the self is, of course, a major area of disagreement between phenomenologists and those who understand consciousness on a behavioral model—that is, consciousness as merely a reaction to outside stimuli. Central to this controversy is the question of whether the self freely directs conscious activity or whether it is merely reacting to forces over which it has no control. The way this question is answered has major implications for all human relationships. Is one responsible for what he does? Can a person be judged for the choices he makes? In short, is man free in his actions?

FREEDOM AND THE WILL

The freewill question is one of the oldest philosophical problems, and it is especially crucial in current thought because of the pervasiveness of the behavioral model of human action. Basic to behaviorism is the view that every action is simply a response to a stimulus, and the relationship between the stimulus and the response is a causal one. A further implication of this view is that human behavior, in principle if not in practice, is as predictable as any other natural event. Behaviorism also claims that human behavior can be accounted for on the basis of the sum total of stimuli and responses, and this would imply that freedom is an illusion resulting from ignorance of the "laws" that govern human behavior.

All of this is antithetical to the phenomenological point of view. In accordance with the phenomenological method, all such explanations must be bracketed in order that full attention may be directed toward an investigation of the phenomenon of will itself, not in contrived laboratory experiments but on the basis of lived-situations. One result of such an investigation is the discovery that will is not a separate faculty or a particular characteristic of a fixed entity; it is rather a complex of conscious activities which, like all conscious activity, is intentionally oriented. The most extensive phenomenological study of the will is the massive two-volume work by Paul Ricoeur entitled *Philosophie de la volonté* (Philosophy of the Will).[3] Ricoeur's analysis points up the fact that willing is a matrix of conscious acts involving a project, which gives rise to motives, deliberation, and decision. The intentional structure of will is seen most clearly in the project itself, which is a future possibility, or set of possibilities, towards which one orients his activity and in light of which one interprets the present situation. In short, the project is any intended action not presently given. Thus, consciousness, in the act of willing, does not determine itself with reference to the surrounding environment alone, nor is it determined by it. The project is rather an orientation to future possibilities which consciousness itself has opened. These future possibilities are themselves the motivating factors in human action; thus, consciousness in its volitional activity is self-determining.

In the traditional discussions of will, deliberation was seen as a choice between two fixed goals. In the phenomenological view, deliberation is the very process of opening up possibilities for choice. The notion of *possibility* is crucial here, for the possible is that which is within one's power: the "I can" precedes the "I will." That is to say, within any action one can analyze the voluntary and involuntary aspects of that action. The voluntary aspect of any decision is anything within the range of possibilities for the self, and seeing the importance of the notion of possibility prevents a distortion of the phenomenological view. Partially as the result of Sartre's somewhat one-sided analysis of freedom, with its claim that man is totally free, the phenomenological view is often misunderstood as saying that any free choice is arbitrary. But Sartre, in his later works, pointed out the situatedness of freedom, which is another way of stressing that the voluntary is always limited to a range of possibilities within a given situation.

But the important aspect of the phenomenological view of freedom is that although every action is situated in a particular historical, social, and physical context, no situation is ever completely closed. Even in the case of a paraplegic, whose actions might be interpreted as having been "determined" by his deficiency, the phenomenological view of the will would point to the many possibilities still open to him among which he may freely choose. Even a serious physical disability does not destroy one's freedom.

But the question of voluntary action can never be raised apart from the situation in which the activity arises; there is always the involuntary pole of any action, which constitutes the background in which choices are made. What is possible within one situation may not be possible in

3. Ricoeur's two-volume work appears in English translation in three volumes. *See* nos. 203, 301, 290.

another. The voluntary as well as the involuntary aspects of choice must be considered within the context of will, for they are the two poles of any decision. Both voluntarism and determinism must be rejected because of the one-sidedness of their analysis.

One aspect of the involuntary pole of any decision is one's body. As has already been mentioned, phenomenology sees consciousness as embodied consciousness, not as separate mental substance or a "ghost in a machine." The body is therefore the mode of one's being in the world and the organ for actualizing conscious intentions in the world. For this reason, the analysis of body and its activity in the world is important for a phenomenological understanding of consciousness and its situatedness.

BODY AND
THE WORLD

The English language has only one word for body, which does not adequately express the different realities to which it refers. Natural science uses the term body to refer to a physical object which can be described in terms of its mass, velocity, and position. When science thus speaks of bodies, it is referring to objects which can be measured, quantified, and described in accordance with mechanical laws. The human body obviously exhibits some of the same characteristics as do other natural bodies. Its weight, size, and motion in relation to other objects can be measured, and its activity can be partially accounted for in terms of physical laws. Phenomenology does not reject such explanations but shows their limitations as complete accounts of human behavior. As in the case of previous examples, phenomenology here too argues against any reductionistic tendency which would reduce all explanations about the body to physical explanations, as would be the case if one affirms that the body is nothing but the total of its observable and measurable operations. Phenomenology argues that the human body cannot merely be understood as another thing in nature or an object among physical objects such as trees, stones, and stars, for the reason that the body of a person is that from which and by means of which all such natural objects are experienced.

Other languages are able to encompass this additional aspect of the meaning of body. German speaks of *Körper* in contrast to *Leib; Körper* refers to a physical object while *Leib* signifies the body which one lives and experiences. Corresponding to this, German also makes a distinction between the experience of the body which one lives *(Erlebnis)* and the experience of an object which one encounters *(Erkenntnis)*. French makes the same distinction in the terms *vécu* ("lived-experience") and *expérience* ("experience of a detached sort"). Phenomenology insists upon the importance of this distinction in order to investigate the aspects of the lived-body which are closed to the quantifying methods of natural science. In order to express these distinctions in English, the term "lived-body" (corresponding to the French *corps propre*) and "lived-experience" are used to distinguish the phenomenological investigation of body from the scientific investigation of it.

One becomes aware of the body that one lives (that is, one's own body) in a way totally different from one's awareness of natural bodies in the scientific sense. The phenomenological investigation of the lived-body begins with one's direct experience of the lived-body and points out the following distinguishing characteristics:

Lived-Body a Center
of Orientation

The lived-body is the center from which everything else is observed. One can never view his lived-body as another object due to the fact that the lived-body is the necessary condition for any experience whatsoever. Everything in the world is seen from the perspective and situatedness of one's own body; the lived-body thus constitutes an irreducible standpoint for any natural experience. Some phenomenologists, for example Paul Ricoeur, refer to the body as the "here from which" (the *ici d'où*) of all perception. But it must not be understood just in the spatial sense (although it includes this meaning) but rather in the broader sense of the center of active orientation.

Lived-Body a Source
of Motives

The lived-body is also a source of motivations for actions, since vital needs, which include the natural requirements for life, enter into all human projects. One may indeed be able to exert some voluntary control over vital needs, but they form a background for all action which can never be totally ignored. They are part and parcel of one's experienced situation. But even vital needs cannot be described totally objectively inasmuch as they are experienced directly. Vital needs show the intimate link between consciousness and the lived-body, but they must be seen within the context of a total human situation.

Lived-Body the Organ
of Action

The lived-body is also the means by which consciousness experiences the world and the means by which it is situated in space and time. And it is only through the body that conscious intentions can be actualized in the world. The body, in fact, is intimately connected with the intentionality of consciousness, since without the lived-body there would be no means for consciousness to be related to the world. This gives added weight to the view that the notion of intentionality must be expanded to include actions as well as thoughts. Actions are always directed toward the world. Consciousness and the body are inseparably linked, and one cannot be understood apart from the other.

Lived-Body Transcended
in the Project

Traditional philosophy overlooked the importance of the lived-body due to the fact that the body is always transcended as a point from which everything else appears. The body, as one's orientation to the world, is always assumed in every project; it is so implicit in every human action that it can only be grasped by a kind of second order of reflection. One way this happens is when the project breaks down, as for example when an athlete fails to perform a desired maneuver in accordance with his project of winning. Here attention is forced back on the body which was always in the background but was usually transcended in favor of the project itself. Phenomenology insists that to understand the body as lived-body, it is always necessary to interpret it in light of the present project. Seen from the vantage point of lived-experience, the action of the lived-body is the correlate of the given situation.

The Lived-Body and Other
Persons

The lived-body is the means by which one is aware of other persons, and in turn the body of others is their way of being present. The consciousness of an individual is expressed through the action of his lived-body, and one's awareness of another person is correlated with one's experience of the other's body. A radical distinction between consciousness and the body (as Descartes made) would provide no way of understanding the other person as embodied consciousness. Husserl investigated the role of the body in one's awareness of other persons in the second volume of *Ideen* (*see* no. 15) and *Cartesian Meditations* (*see* no. 24) by using the concept of analogy and apperception. He meant to distinguish one's knowledge of the other person from one's knowledge of a physical object. One experiences the other as embodied consciousness, not as a mere object in nature, for one sees the other as analogous to oneself. The phenomenological investigation of the body has been continued by the work of Merleau-Ponty and Paul Ricoeur.

The upshot of the phenomenological analysis of the body is that the lived-body is one's only access to the world, and the world cannot even be considered apart from the perspective offered by the body. Hence, the role of perception in world understanding is likewise an important phenomenological theme.

PERCEPTION

The distinguishing features of the phenomenological view of perception can best be seen when contrasted with the traditional view which is dominated by the causal model. In this view the mind is understood as an organism (usually thought of as a passive receptacle for sensations) causally related to physical objects. The physical object emits or reflects waves and particles which impinge on the brain and are then translated into a copy of the object being experienced.

The phenomenological analysis of perception admits that there is a causal link between the organism and the object which is being experienced, but it insists that perception involves more than this. In line with its method, phenomenology goes directly to the experience of perception itself and in doing so points out a major difficulty with the causal model of perception. Science would describe sound, for example, as the movement of energy waves transmitted by the particles of air which impinge upon the organic structures of the ear and are thus transmitted to the brain. But this kind of explanation leaves out the most important part, namely the sound itself. For one does not experience the movement of particles in the air or the organic process described by science but rather the *sound* of Beethoven's Ninth Symphony, for example. A physical description of the instruments in the orchestra and a physical account of the action of the ear are inadequate to account for the sound of the symphony. Sound certainly involves these aspects, but as a phenomenon it cannot be fully accounted for on these terms alone.

Viewed phenomenologically, perception is seen as intentional; that is, perception is always perception of . . . . This means that in perception the structures of perception themselves are not given. What is given is the perceived object in the world. To investigate the perception in terms of its organic makeup is to already assume a perception which investigates both. Perception, therefore, can never be investigated as an object, for it is on the basis of perception that all objects appear. Seen as a phenomenon, however, a perception involves much more than what many contemporary thinkers refer to as "sense data." The sense data are indeed an important part of the perception, but they are never given as such. One does not experience sense data but an object having characteristics which themselves are not sense data. Sense data, in order to be a perception and have meaning, must be organized, synthesized, and unified in terms of the intended object. In this activity, retention, imagination, anticipation, and memory are as important to the meaning of perception as is the causal relationship between the sense organ and the object being perceived.

One of the dilemmas of the traditional explanation of perception was how one can compare the sense data with the object being perceived. If sense data are viewed as providing a kind of copy of the physical object, and all one ever knows are sense data, then one can never correlate the copy with the perceived object. Phenomenology avoids this problem by refusing to make a radical separation between the act of perception and the object perceived. Since perception, like all conscious acts, is intentional, there is no perception apart from the object being perceived. For phenomenology, then, the object is as it is perceived. The distance between the world and the self is bridged, and the problems of empiricism and idealism are avoided. One's awareness of the world is immediate and always assumed by any theoretical explanation whatsoever, be it empiricist or idealist. The problem generated by the empiricist theory of perception was how the experienced world is related to the real world. For the phenomenologist, the perceived world is the real world.

VALUES

The empiricist also has difficulty accounting for values, since values are not experienced according to the empiricist's criteria. For the radical empiricist, the only kind of *objectivity* is the spatio-temporal sphere, that is, objects which can be measured and quantified. From the empiricist point of view, the only aspect of values which can be so treated are the human responses to them, and the temptation is to reduce all accounts of values to the empirical state of the human subject. To be more specific, one current interpretation of values is that they are merely human expressions of like and dislike, approval and disapproval, and are analyzable in terms of psychological states. On this account, a person's statement, "honesty is good," is reducible to the statement, "I approve of honesty," or "hoorah for honesty." Similarly, the statement "the sunset is beautiful" is reducible to "I like the sunset." Or the assertion, "I ought to tell the truth" can be reduced to "truth telling gives me pleasure." All such attempts to explain values are manifestations of a subjectivistic position which is analogous to the psychologistic attempt to reduce logic to subjective states. Hence, phenomenology responds with the same type of critique of this psychologistic interpretation of values as it does to the psychologistic interpretation of logic. Phenomenology insists that just as logical axioms cannot be reduced to psychological states, neither can values—whether ethical or esthetic—be explained entirely in terms of psychological states.

The current subjectivistic interpretation of values constitutes a vast literature and involves a variety of views which are too extensive to be surveyed here. But the basic presupposition common to all subjectivistic views is that values are projections of life's needs, whether physical or emotional. On this view the values of the good and the beautiful are explainable in terms of what gives pleasure; the evil and the ugly are derivable from that which produces pain. Or values may be explained in terms of subconscious states, libidinal impulses, or as the compensations of suppressed drives. Common to all varieties of such interpretations is that values are not objective in any sense, and it is this basic presupposition that phenomenology challenges.

As the preceding discussion of phenomenology has stressed, every conscious state is conscious of something. The object is the correlate of the conscious activity, and phenomenology recognizes many different kinds of objectivity corresponding to different levels of consciousness. The basic criticism of subjectivism, according to phenomenology, is that it takes only one side of this duality, emphasizing the subjective state without attending to the objective correlate toward which the subjective state is directed and from which it derives its meaning. The reason subjectivistic value theory failed to recognize the objectivity of values is due to the limited meaning given to objectivity in its view, namely, that the only kind of objectivity is spatio-temporal. By pointing out that every conscious state has its objective correlate, phenomenology shows that different levels of conscious experience have different areas of objectivity.

Phenomenology also shows that an experience of value is always an experience of something given to consciousness, and the value is not experienced as a projection, a vital need, or an emotion. All of these subjective states are interpreted in terms of an already-experienced value; in fact, the distinction between which emotion refers to which value assumes a prior awareness of the value. Edmund Husserl presented a number of seminars in value theory, which unfortunately are not yet published, although an account of them is given by Alois Roth (*see* no. 93). A rigorous criticism of the subjectivistic attempt to reduce values to principles of pleasure and pain is given by Paul Ricoeur in the context of his phenomenological treatment of the will.[4]

Ethical theory is concerned with such concepts as responsibility and choice, duty, obligation, and relationships to the other person. These are subjects already referred to in the preceding discussion, but it must be stressed that the phenomenological view of ethics is based on the priority of freedom and the responsibility which accrues to the author of free choices. And as Kant argued, the notions of duty and obligation are meaningless terms without freedom. Phenomenology continues this Kantian tradition but adds to it the demonstration that freedom is the basic constitution of human consciousness. Interpersonal relationships also occupy a central position in the phenomenological analysis of ethics, which again continues the Kantian emphasis upon the respect of a rational creature for other rational beings. The basic criterion in the choice among values is the respect of and the responsibility to the other person as a center of valuating activity.

Although stemming from an early period in the development of phenomenology, a significant analysis of ethics from the phenomenological viewpoint is offered in the work of Max Scheler, one of Husserl's coworkers. In one of his major works on ethics, *Formalism in Ethics and Non-Formal Ethics of Values* (*see* no. 224), Scheler showed the inadequacies of Kant's ethical formalism. His tactic was the same as that Husserl had used in his attack upon psychologism—namely, an exposition of the presuppositions and the limitations lying behind formalism. Scheler claimed, however, that his work was not a refutation of Kant but a phenomenological investigation of moral experience which consists of an immediate "seeing-into" (intuition) its essence as pure phenomenon. Moral experience is simply given, and as such is neither universal nor individual. The moral phenomenon does not arise from combining a multiplicity to form a commonality, for such a combination already presupposes an intuition of its essence. In short, the act of intuition and the object intuited form an indissoluble phenomenological fact *(Tatsache)*. Hence, phenomenology seeks to reveal the pregiven essences of moral experiences and their relationships. This approach also reveals Scheler's view of the nature of philosophy. Philosophy, he claimed, is a "spiritual" process or activity because only spirit can act; everything else merely "functions." In fact, Scheler claimed that the activity of philosophizing is not relegated to professionals but constitutes the very core of human personhood. Man is not free to philosophize or not. He always does so whether consciously or through inheriting his philosophy from his tradition.

4. Ricoeur, *Freedom and Nature*, pp. 99–134. *See* no. 203.

Spirit is pure actuality, and its very being is not a substance but a continuously self-executing, ordered structure of acts. The person is only in and through his acts. An additional point must also be stressed: spirit does not possess faculties or characteristics such as reason or vitality. Spirit is an immediate coexperiencing unity of all lived experiences; hence it is concrete and not formal. Spiritual acts are experienced only in their enactment and can never become intentional objects for formal investigation. Against Kant, Scheler maintained that the moral autonomy of a person is not a "law-rule" (*Logonomie*) of pure reason, nor can it become a logical subject of propositions. This allows Scheler to make a distinction between formal principles, which deal with an objectified logical structure, and ethical principles, which belong in the sphere of person or spirit.

Scheler further showed the irreducibility of ethics to formal principles. Moral values manifest themselves in affective phenomena, which make up an independent and permanent realm of values. Against the formalists and rationalists, Scheler defended the "order of the heart" of Pascal in dealing with the a priori structures of affective values. Emotional values place man in direct contact with the real, the vital, and the concrete. Hence, a philosophical study of this sphere seeks to reveal the essences of values. Such a study describes the intentional direction and content within the experiencing act as it is elicited by its own end. The response to material values puts man in direct contact with the vital sphere of life, which is the basic core of the real and to which all the levels—the vegetative, the sentient, and the spiritual—must respond. The error of rationalism is that it had lost all contact with the vital and real. This same point can be made with reference to metaphysics vis-à-vis religion. Metaphysical knowledge is formal and abstract and possesses only an ideal, cerebral God of the intellectuals; religious experience places one in a vital communion with the absolute.

As has already been mentioned, there is, for Scheler, a vital sphere which comprises all the functions of life. Spirit can say "No" to the vital and can refuse to be reduced to it, yet the vital is required for all the activity of the spirit in that without the vital, spirit would be lifeless. The spiritual emerges within the vital and gains its strength by opposing the vital. Here man is one with two irreducible moments: impulse and spirit. In itself, spirit is lacking all energy, yet vital factors by themselves lead only to chaos. Spirit, therefore, has a dual task: a negative one wherein spirit must restrain, control, and inhibit; a positive one in which spirit directs and guides the impulses of the vital sphere. Spiritual ideas, to be realized, must be incorporated into the vital sphere, for they depend on the energy of this sphere for their realization.

Scheler's discussion of the intentionality of emotions, their metaphysical significance, and their laws of dependence, allows him to deal with the ideal and normative order of values. One ideal that he proposes is the cultivation of the emotional powers to realize ideals. This means that his main concern was to reunite man with his vital powers which, although lower in the scale of values, are the most powerful. Man would undermine his existence if he cultivated only formal values. Love, sympathy, and benevolence are required to temper Kant's empty formalism. But the primary value is man's spirit which transcends nature and yet which, when united with nature, yields the full experience of man, his relationships with other men, and his relationship with God. Hence, moral value is found in "fellow feeling" which reveals the fact that emotional intentionality has positive ethical value: a sorrow shared is a sorrow halved; a joy shared is a joy doubled.

The lowest values are the sensory feelings of the pleasant and the unpleasant. In this area there cannot be any genuine love. One cannot love sunshine; it can only give pleasure or pain. The value of such feelings cannot lead to the realization of higher potentialities. Vital values, which are at a higher level, are those of health, vigor, and nobility; hence the love of authentic friendship, family, and noble deeds. Vital values institute a bond in all living community and give rise to the respect and love of all life.

Spiritual values are the esthetic, juridical, and epistemic values which illuminate the lower values and tie humans in mental relations, educational advances, and cultural creations. They constitute the very bonds and fabric of society. Religious values are the highest and deal with the holy and unholy and are related to the emotions of bliss, worship, and awe. Religious values constitute the spiritual love of persons and generate "moral love" and knowledge of a common life and salvation.

All these values, however, deal with the value of persons. The other person is irreducible to anything except an absolute, concrete center of spiritual acts. Scheler's conclusion is that the personal values of others, and God as the source of values, are the absolute foundation for all other values. Scheler's special contribution centers in showing man's emotional relationship to values and in his insistence that values are not subjective or locked up in the "inner man." Emotions are meaningful and intentional with values as their objects (*Wertfühlen*).

Esthetics, from the phenomenological point of view, brackets the empirical and psychologistic interpretation of a work of art and focuses on the immediately experienced aspects of the work. A merely empirical description, which attended only to the color, shape, size, tonal quality, and other measurable characteristics of the work, will not account for the experience of the nobility of the portrait or the experienced harmony of the symphony. In short, the esthetic object has its own area of objectivity not reducible either to empirical descriptions of the physical object or the psychological states and reactions of the observer. A poem cannot be explained totally in terms of the sounds of the words comprising it or the marks on the paper; these empirical aspects are the bearers of the meaning of the poem, but the poem's meaning is not identical with these empirical characteristics. If one judges that the words of a poem are inadequate, or that the poem itself is a poor poem, he is doing so on the assumption that there is a prior value by which the poem is judged. The same principle can be applied to any esthetic judgment. In sum, phenomenology insists upon the *meaning* of the esthetic experience, which, like all conscious activity, has its objective as well as subjective correlate. To isolate either from the other is to falsify the experience by giving it a one-sided interpretation.

LANGUAGE

From Husserl's *Logical Investigations* to Heidegger's *On the Way to Language* to Merleau-Ponty's *Phenomenology of Perception,* language has played a major role in phenomenological investigation. This aspect of phenomenology is especially of current interest because of the centrality of language analysis in Anglo-American philosophy, which stresses the function of language in formal systems. Through their interest in language, many philosophers of both the phenomenological and analytic type hope to find a common point of contact between these diverse philosophical views.

Basic to the phenomenological view of language is an emphasis upon its intentional structure. Language is always about . . . , just as consciousness is always consciousness of . . . . Language is an expression of conscious intentionality in terms of meaning. Being the basic mode of expression of the intentional structure of consciousness, language understood phenomenologically includes all the ways consciousness expresses its relation to the world. The gesture, the look, bodily stances, as well as formal systems of communication must be included in the notion of language. But as an example of the phenomenological view of language, the following discussion will focus on the spoken and written word.

Language, understood as spoken or written expression, comprises two aspects—the empirical dimension and the sphere of meaning, which are never given one without the other. The empirical aspect of language includes sounds and visual marks, whereas the meaning of language is that which is expressed through sounds and visual signs. It is a mistake, however, to equate the meaning of language with the arbitrary system of signs constituting that language. The meaning of any spoken or written expression is not reducible to such a system, for different systems may express the same meaning, or different meanings may be expressed by the same system. Whereas a given system consists only of a finite number of sounds or visual signs, it can express an infinite number of meanings. From a phenomenological point of view, language is never closed but, like consciousness itself, is open to an infinite number of possibilities.

In analyzing language, phenomenology deals not only with the formal language system itself but with the intended meaning, which is always directed to something other than language. This has led, particularly in the work of Heidegger, to the notion of language as *logos* (the Greek term for "word"). As *logos,* language is the bearer of meanings, and these meanings are meanings about the world that are grasped by consciousness. Language, however, cannot be understood in an abstract sense but only in its concrete situation. A single word in isolation from its context has no meaning; the meaning of the word dervies its unity from the total situation, which includes the outward expression as well as the objective context. In short, language, like consciousness, is always situated. The situatedness of language is a life-situation, not a series of lexical meanings as one would find in a dictionary, for the situation in which language functions prescribes what the words of language mean. Lexical meanings are defined with reference to the meanings of other words in what is essentially a closed system. But in experience, one finds that language is not a closed system, for with a finite number of signs (letters, sounds, grammatical rules) one can express an infinite number of meanings. This kind of analysis shows that the possibility of new meanings arises out of the lived-situation. Failure to take this lived-situation into one's account of language will not give a full understanding of language as it is experienced. In short, phenomenology finds the meaning of language in the context of "worldly" situations as they are lived.

ONTOLOGY AND METAPHYSICS

A final area of philosophical investigation is the inquiry into the ultimate nature of reality, or metaphysics as it has been traditionally called. The question of metaphysics has remained a continuing problem in traditional philosophy as a result of the assumption that the subject is capable of knowing only appearances. The problem of how one knows the nature of reality as it is in itself remained a perpetual puzzle and a stumbling block which led Kant to assert that metaphysics, in the traditional sense, is impossible. A corollary to this Kantian view is that whenever reason attempts metaphysical speculation, it falls into confusion and contradiction.

Phenomenology bypasses this cul de sac by demonstrating that reality is as it is experienced. But the term *experience* must be taken in the broad sense that encompasses any possible object of which one is conscious. Each level of experience demands its own principles of understanding, and it is phenomenology's task to make explicit what these principles are. (For further discussion of this aspect of phenomenology, see the relevant sections of chapter 3 dealing with regional ontologies.) But the question of ultimate reality is not answerable in that form, for ultimate reality is not an object given to immediate intuition. It can only be approached by degrees in the process of transcending each partial perspective. What this comes down to, especially for Heidegger and Jaspers, is that the ultimate metaphysical question is the question of Being. For Heidegger (as well as for Jaspers) the question of Being cannot be answered in terms of the subject-object relationship but must be approached by way of the limits of traditional metaphysics.

The question of Being, or "fundamental ontology" as it is usually referred to, is what Heidegger calls a forgotten question. He charges that, since the time of Plato, Western philosophy has understood Being as only an entity among entities, albeit the highest entity. In fact, the very term *ultimate reality* betrays this prejudice, for this expression reveals no real difference between *reality* and *Being* conceived as the *ultimate* reality. This gave rise to what Lovejoy called the great chain of Being, a hierarchy of increasing perfections with nothingness at the bottom and Being at the top as its ultimate expression. But this chain of Being seems to be nothing more than an arrangement of entities from lowest to highest without the realization that Being (in Heidegger's sense) is not the highest entity but belongs to all entities and yet is different from them. For Heidegger, this difference is crucial, for whenever we think or speak we find ourselves assuming the difference. Whenever we say that something is, was, or will be, we are already distinguishing between something and *that* it is. This means, for Heidegger, that things appear in the light of Being but in such a way that their being is also temporal; that is, the terms *is, was,* or *will be* signify temporal dimensions of Being not reducible to any particular object or subject. Hence, time becomes crucial for understanding Being, whereas traditional metaphysics placed Being beyond all temporal processes.

The upshot of Heidegger's fundamental ontology is that to understand Being one must grasp the difference between Being and being, and this difference is found in the place where Being manifests itself. For Heidegger this is *Dasein* ("being-there"), which he understands as ex-istence. As has already been mentioned in the brief discussion of Heidegger in chapter 4, *Dasein* is the term he reserves for human ex-istence, understood in its etymological sense (hence the hyphenated form) as "going out" toward Being. Human *Dasein* is, in other words, openness to Being and is the place where Being manifests itself.

Heidegger's approach is not the only phenomenological investigation of ontology, for Karl Jaspers, Jean-Paul Sartre, and Maurice Merleau-Ponty have also attempted to elaborate phenomenological ontologies. Since a brief discussion of Sartre and Jaspers has already been included in chapter 4, an examination of Merleau-Ponty's novel approach to ontology will illustrate the variations on this theme that are nevertheless still within the framework of the phenomenological method.

For Merleau-Ponty, Being—which he calls "savage Being"—is given in perception. Each perceivable object may be understood in light of one significance, but this significance does not exhaust that object. And in perceptual experience one may continue to go into the depth of significances without exhausting them in the object. A perception of a color, for example, appears not only as colored but as warm, soft, attracting and so on into an inexhaustible depth. Thus, every object is crisscrossed with a multitude of significances which can be traced out perceptually but never exhausted. There is no final resting point in perceptual experience; since perceptual experience is never exhausted, it is exhausting to the perceiver who is moved without end continuously to investigate perceived Being. Hence the term *savage Being* points to this endless pursuit of the meaning of perceptual experience. For Merleau-Ponty, meaning is the inexhaustible matrix within which things are cradled and which perception assumes in order to be meaningful. There can no longer be the claim that the world is meaningless (as nihilism would have it), for every perceptual experience is filled with inexhaustible dimensions of meaning.

The very variety of phenomenological ontologies attests to the fact that phenomenology rejects any comprehensive system of metaphysics that would subsume all reality under one category or set of categories, for any such group of principles are never given in their totality but only partially and from a given perspective, which always leaves them open for further investigation. Prior assumptions, theories, and explanations must be bracketed and can become valid only if they can be authenticated in lived-experience. For the claim common to all phenomenological ontologies is that lived-experience is the place where Being makes itself known.

BIBLIOGRAPHY

Many of the subheads in the following bibliography are somewhat arbitrary inasmuch as most of the works cited defy narrow classification. Each of the headings, however, reflects an area of discussion in the chapter, and the works included are some of the major studies available. No effort was made to separate English from non-English works, and journal articles were included only when they added a significant dimension to the topic. Annotations are provided when the title of the work does not provide a reasonable idea of the contents.

Consciousness and the Self

192. Berger, Gaston. *The Cogito in Husserl's Philosophy*. Translated by Kathleen McLaughlin. Evanston, Ill.: Northwestern Univ. Pr., 1972.

193. Edie, James M.; Parker, Francis H.; and Schrag, Calvin O., eds. *Patterns of the Life-World: Essays in Honor of John Wild*. Evanston, Ill.: Northwestern Univ. Pr., 1970.
    Collection of articles by leading phenomenologists discussing the life-world and various approaches to it, including the problem of subjectivity and objectivity.

194. Embree, Lester E., ed. *Life-World and Consciousness: Essays for Aron Gurwitsch*. Evanston, Ill.: Northwestern Univ. Pr., 1972.
    Articles by leading phenomenologists dealing with three areas: consciousness, its structure, and the methods leading to its investigation; language and Gestalt theories; and problems of the life-world.

195. Farber, Marvin. *Naturalism and Subjectivism*. Springfield, Ill.: Thomas, 1959.
    Deals with transcendental consciousness and its relationship to the natural world; shows the distinct area of human spirit by way of Max Scheler's philosophy. Good bibliography.

196. Gurwitsch, Aron. *Field of Consciousness*. Pittsburgh: Duquesne Univ. Pr., 1964.
    Deals with the phenomenological concept of consciousness and its consequent theory of perception.

197. ———. *Studies in Phenomenology and Psychology*. Evanston, Ill.: Northwestern Univ. Pr., 1966.
    Critique of the psychological theories of William James and Gestalt psychology and concluding with a phenomenological theory of consciousness.

198. Husserl, Gerhart. *Person, Sache, Verhalten*. Frankfort: Vittorio Klostermann, 1970.
    Shows the structure of human personality, the structure of natural things, and the relationship between the two.

199. Sartre, Jean-Paul. *Being and Nothingness*. Translated by Hazel E. Barnes. New York: Philosophical Library, 1956.

Sartre's major philosophical work in which he develops his theory of consciousness, its relation to Being, the body, and the world; on the basis of his "phenomenological ontology" he shows the radical nature of human freedom.

200. ———. *The Transcendence of the Ego: An Existential Theory of Consciousness.* Translated by Forrest Williams and Robert Kirkpatrick. New York: Noonday, 1957.

Shows that prereflective consciousness is nonegological, and upon reflection the ego arises as the past project of consciousness.

Also see nos. 15, 16, 24, 29, 47, 80.

Freedom and the Will

201. Berdyaev, Nicolas. *Freedom and the Spirit.* Translated by Olive Fielding Clarke. New York: Scribner, 1935.

Shows that the notion of freedom cannot be understood apart from reference to spirit and that spirit cannot be limited by any definition.

202. ———. *Slavery and Freedom.* Translated by R. M. French. New York: Scribner, 1960.

Deals with the various forms of enslavement from those of the ego itself to the enslaving forces of culture.

203. Ricoeur, Paul. *Freedom and Nature: The Voluntary and the Involuntary.* Translated by Erazim V. Kohák. Evanston, Ill.: Northwestern Univ. Pr., 1966.

Analysis of the structures of the will which give rise to voluntary action and set its limits. Translation of volume one of *Philosophie de la volonté.*

204. Sartre, Jean-Paul. *Existentialism.* Translated by Bernard Frechtman. New York: Philosophical Library, 1947.

Shows the radical nature of human freedom and the responsibility each free choice entails. Translation of an early lecture given by Sartre in 1945 and entitled *"L'Existentialisme est un humanisme,"* which has taken on something of the status of position paper for his atheistic existentialism and is frequently anthologized in various translations under the title "Existentialism Is a Humanism" or "The Humanism of Existentialism."

205. Schrag, Calvin O. *Existence and Freedom: Towards an Ontology of Human Finitude.* Evanston, Ill.: Northwestern Univ. Pr., 1970.

Discusses the existential view of freedom in terms of transitoriness, history, and time.

206. Schulthess, Robert. *Ich-Freiheit-Schicksal.* Tübingen: Max Niemeyer Verlag, 1959.

Shows the structure of the ego and its inclinations with respect to freedom; introduces historical considerations of freedom.

207. Straus, Erwin, and Griffith, Richard, eds. *Phenomenology of Will and Action: Second Lexington Conference on Pure and Applied Phenomenology.* Pittsburgh: Duquesne Univ. Pr., 1967.

Leading authorities in phenomenology and psychology discussing such questions as will, body image, skills, compulsive and fanatic basis of action, and theatrical performance.

Also see nos. 184, 199.

Body and the World

208. Langan, Thomas. *Merleau-Ponty's Critique of Reason.* New Haven: Yale Univ. Pr., 1966.

Deals with Merleau-Ponty's basic notions of perception in relation to the linguistic gesture and phenomenological concept of body.

209. Maier, Werner. *Das Problem der Leiblichkeit bei Jean-Paul Sartre und Maurice Merleau-Ponty.* Tübingen: Max Niemeyer Verlag, 1964.

Analysis of the role of the human body for an understanding of man in the thought of Sartre and Merleau-Ponty.

210. Merleau-Ponty, Maurice. *The Structure of Behavior.* Boston: Beacon, 1963.

Technical and detailed analysis of human anatomy and physiology to show that the theories of localized functions are inadequate not only on a physiological basis but also as adequate accounts of human behavior.

211. Plügge, Herbert. *Der Mensch und sein Leib.* Tübingen: Max Niemeyer Verlag, 1967.

Analysis of different levels of experience and their structures in bodily constitution.

Also see nos. 15, 105, 195, 199, 213.

Perception

212. Asemissen, H. U. *Strukturanalytische Probleme der Wahrnehmung in der Phänomenologie Husserls.* Cologne: Kantstudien Ergänzungsheft 73, 1957.

Delineates the basic problems in Husserl's phenomenology concerning the relationship between empirical, psychological, and transcendental levels of consciousness in terms of perception.

213. Merleau-Ponty, Maurice. *The Phenomenology of Perception*. Translated by Colin Smith. London: Routledge & Kegan Paul, 1962.
     Monumental critique of the theories of perception of empiricism and rationalism.

214. ———. *The Primacy of Perception and Other Essays on Phenomenological Psychology, the Philosophy of Art, History and Politics*. Edited by James M. Edie. Translated by William Cobb et al. Evanston, Ill.: Northwestern Univ. Pr., 1964.
     Title essay provides further insights into Merleau-Ponty's theory of perception.

215. ———. *The Prose of the World*. Translated by John O'Neill. Evanston, Ill.: Northwestern Univ. Pr., 1970.
     Deals with perception of the world in terms of such linguistic modalities as dialogue, indirect language, mystery of language, and the experience of expression.

216. ———. *The Visible and the Invisible*. Translated by Alphonso Lingis. Evanston, Ill.: Northwestern Univ. Pr., 1968.
     Shows that the visible is encompassed by lines of invisible significance and that the invisible context makes sense of visible phenomena.

217. O'Neill, John. *Perception, Expression, and History: The Social Phenomenology of Maurice Merleau-Ponty*. Evanston, Ill.: Northwestern Univ. Pr., 1970.
     Shows that history and culture constitute the basic modes of perception and that conscious structures are identical with the temporally oriented cultural world.

     Also see no. 30.

Values: Ethics

218. Frings, Manfred. *Max Scheler: A Concise Introduction into the World of a Great Thinker*. Pittsburgh: Duquesne Univ. Pr., 1965.
     Analysis of the ethical theories of Max Scheler showing the different levels of human constitution and the priority of love in nonformal ethical values.

219. Frondizi, Risieri. *What Is Value?* 2d ed. La Salle, Ill.: Open Court, 1971.
     Attempt to establish a basis for ethics as a Gestalt quality reducible neither to subjective nor objective interpretation.

220. Hartmann, Nicolai. *Ethics.* Translated by Stanton Coit. New York: Macmillan, 1932.

     Shows the irreducibility of values to any material region, such as economics, psychology, or culture.

221. Mandelbaum, Maurice. *The Phenomenology of Moral Experience.* Baltimore: Johns Hopkins Pr., 1969.

     Analysis of the basis of moral values in lived experience and focusing on the moral region in counterdistinction to other regions of experience.

222. Olafson, Frederick A. *Principles and Persons.* Baltimore: Johns Hopkins Pr., 1967.

     Analysis of values in terms of freedom, choice, action, and obligation, with particular reference to the ethical views of Sartre and Heidegger.

223. Polin, Raymond. *La Création des valeurs. Recherches sur le fondement de l'objectivité axiologique.* Paris: Presses Universitaires de France, 1945.

     Application of the phenomenological epoche to value theory in general and to ethics in particular.

224. Scheler, Max. *Formalism in Ethics and Non-Formal Ethics of Values.* Translated by Manfred S. Frings and Roger L. Funk. Evanston, Ill.: Northwestern Univ. Pr., 1973.

     Massive exposition of values showing their psychological foundation in such experiences as love and resentment and arguing that every human endeavor is based on valuation.

225. ———. *Ressentiment.* Translated by William W. Holdheim. New York: Free Press of Glencoe, 1961.

     Shows how some values arise in a negative way through the psychological states of resentment.

     Also see nos. 93, 152, 204.

Values: Esthetics

226. Berleant, Arnold. *The Aesthetic Field: A Phenomenology of Aesthetic Experience.* Springfield, Ill.: Thomas, 1969.

     Shows the proper object of esthetic creation and the required levels of conscious experience.

227. Hanneborg, Knut. *The Study of Literature: A Contribution to the Phenomenology of the Humane Sciences.* Oslo: Universitetsforlagert, 1967.

     Deals with the methodological problem, attitudes, and philosophical foundations in the study of literature.

228. Heidegger, Martin. "The Origin of the Work of Art." In *Philosophies of Art and Beauty,* edited by Albert Hofstadter and Richard Kuhns, pp. 649–701. New York: Random, Modern Library, 1964.

On the basis of his ontological principles, Heidegger shows that art is an opening of an existential world.

229. Ingarden, Roman. *Das literarische Kunstwerk.* Tübingen: Max Niemeyer Verlag, 1965.

Deals with meaning, its various levels, and its symbolic value in a literary work of art.

230. ———. *Untersuchungen zur Ontologie der Kunst.* Tübingen: Max Niemeyer Verlag, 1962.

Ingarden's essays on music, painting, architecture, and films showing that valuation is basic to the existence of any work of art.

231. ———. *Vom Erkennen des literarischen Kunstwerks.* Tübingen: Max Niemeyer Verlag, 1968.

Analysis of the structure of the art work and its recognition in terms of different linguistic functions and temporal structures.

232. Kaelin, Eugene Francis. *Art and Existence: A Phenomenological Aesthetics.* Lewisburg, Pa.: Bucknell Univ. Pr., 1970.

Analysis of different esthetic areas and their distinguishing structures; extensive bibliography.

233. ———. *An Existential Aesthetic: The Theories of Sartre and Merleau-Ponty.* Madison, Wis.: Univ. of Wisconsin Pr., 1962.

Shows the distinct approaches to esthetic experience by Merleau-Ponty and Sartre, Sartre's being based on negativity and exclusion of empirical factors, Merleau-Ponty's being based on immediate perception.

234. Merleau-Ponty, Maurice. *Signs.* Translated by Richard C. McCleary. Evanston, Ill.: Northwestern Univ. Pr., 1964.

Consideration of artistic and cultural works as signs or indicators of man's relationship to Being.

235. Sartre, Jean-Paul. *Literature and Existentialism.* Translated by Bernard Frechtman. New York: Citadel Pr., 1962.

Shows the importance of the existential consideration of freedom as fundamental for any literary creation.

236. ———. *What Is Literature?* Translated by Bernard Frechtman. New York: Harper & Row, 1965.

Deals with the questions of the value of writing, the public for which one writes, and the situations in which one writes.

237. Straus, Erwin, and Griffith, Richard, eds. *Aisthesis and Aesthetics: Fourth Lexington Conference on Pure and Applied Phenomenology*. Pittsburgh: Duquesne Univ. Pr., 1970.
     Contributors from phenomenology and different esthetic fields deal with the perception of esthetic objects.

238. Tymieniecka, Anna-Teresa, ed. *For Roman Ingarden: Nine Essays in Phenomenology*. The Hague: Martinus Nijhoff, 1959.
     Collection of articles by various phenomenologists dealing with a variety of subjects, including esthetics.

     Also see nos. 66, 214.

Language

239. Derrida, Jacques. *Speech and Phenomena, and Other Essays on Husserl's Theory of Signs*. Translated by David B. Allison. Evanston, Ill.: North-western Univ. Pr., 1973.
     Discussion of the different dimensions in language and a discussion of the shortcomings of Husserl's philosophy of language.

240. Erickson, Stephen A. *Language and Being: An Analytic Phenomenology*. New Haven: Yale Univ. Pr., 1970.
     Analysis of Heidegger's notion of language in relation to the question of Being and its meaning.

241. Heidegger, Martin. *On the Way to Language*. Translated by Peter D. Hertz. New York: Harper & Row, 1971.
     Deals with language as *logos* reflecting, in authentic discourse, the structure of the world.

242. Heintel, Erich. *Einführung in die Sprachphilosophie*. Darmstadt: Wissenschaftliche Buchgesellschaft, 1972.
     Discusses the current linguistic questions from phenomenological and hermeneutical perspectives and presents an excellent bibliography of contemporary European work in language theory.

243. Hems, John M. "Husserl and/or Wittgenstein." *International Philosophical Quarterly* 8 (1968):547–78.
     Analysis of common problems and areas of interest in the thought of Husserl and Wittgenstein showing possible points of contact between phenomenology and language philosophy.

244. Kockelmans, Joseph J., ed. and trans. *On Heidegger and Language*. Evanston, Ill.: Northwestern Univ. Pr., 1972.

Contains papers presented at the International Colloquim on Heidegger's conception of language (1969).

245. Kwant, Remy C. *Phenomenology of Expression.* Translated by Henry J. Koren. Pittsburgh: Duquesne Univ. Pr., 1969.

Deals with all modalities of human expression, of which spoken language is one instance.

246. Mays, Wolfe, and Brown, S. C. *Linguistic Analysis and Phenomenology.* Lewisburg, Pa.: Bucknell Univ. Pr., 1972.

Deals with questions such as freedom and determinism, esthetics, body and mind, and philosophical method from the perspectives of linguistic analysis and phenomenology. Contributors are leading philosophers who presented these papers at the Philosophers into Europe Conference, University of Southampton, 1969.

Also see nos. 208, 213, 215, 216.

Ontology and Metaphysics

247. Carlo, William E. *The Ultimate Reducibility of Essence to Existence in Existential Metaphysics.* The Hague: Martinus Nijhoff, 1966.

Argues that the essential structures of human existence, although intimately connected to the factual human situation, are not derivable from it.

248. Fink, Eugen. *Zur ontologischen Frühgeschichte von Raum-Zeit-Bewegung.* The Hague: Martinus Nijhoff, 1957.

Phenomenological approach to the ontological status of space, time, and motion.

249. Heidegger, Martin. *Being and Time.* Translated by John Macquarrie and Edward Robinson. New York: Harper & Row, 1962.

Heidegger's major work in which he develops his own critique of the way Western philosophy has dealt with the structures of man's being-in-the-world in its relation to Being.

250. ———. *An Introduction to Metaphysics.* Translated by Ralph Manheim. New Haven: Yale Univ. Pr., 1959.

Shows the origins of the question of Being and how in the philosophic tradition this has been reduced to questions about physical nature.

251. Landgrebe, Ludwig. *Phänomenologie und Metaphysik.* Hamburg: Marion von Schröner Verlag, 1949.

Argues against life-philosophy as inadequate for understanding human experience and attempts to point the way to ontology through phenomenology.

252. Luijpen, William A. *Phenomenology and Metaphysics*. Translated by Henry J. Koren. Pittsburgh: Duquesne Univ. Pr., 1965.

Gives a scholastic interpretation of phenomenology and argues for the possibility of metaphysics in a more traditional sense.

253. Marcel, Gabriel. *The Mystery of Being*. 2 vols. Translated by G. S. Fraser and René Hague. Chicago: Regnery, 1960.

Marcel's Gifford lectures in which he makes the distinction between problem and mystery and shows that Being is a mystery of incarnate existence.

254. Scheler, Max. *Man's Place in Nature*. Translated by Hans Meyerhoff. Boston: Beacon, 1961.

Deals with the levels of reality and values and shows man's relationship to those levels.

255. ———. *Selected Philosophical Essays*. Translated by David R. Lachterman. Evanston, Ill.: Northwestern Univ. Pr., 1972.

Scheler's works in epistemology, metaphysics, and philosophical psychology.

256. Schrag, Calvin O. *Experience and Being: Prolegomena to a Future Ontology*. Evanston, Ill.: Northwestern Univ. Pr., 1969.

An attempt to develop a new philosophy of experience in dialogue with thinkers both in the existential and phenomenological traditions such as Kierkegaard, Nietzsche, Husserl, Heidegger, and Merleau-Ponty.

257. Sontag, Frederick. *Existentialist Prolegomena: To a Future Metaphysics*. Chicago: Univ. of Chicago Pr., 1969.

Deals with the basis of all metaphysical knowledge in relation to psychological and literary experience and introduces the questions of time and nothingness.

258. Thibault, Herve J. *Creation and Metaphysics: A Genetic Approach to Existential Act*. The Hague: Martinus Nijhoff, 1970.

Shows that the creative act is irreducible to any material conditions and that ultimately creation in the metaphysical sense is a free act of God.

Also see nos. 86, 89, 92, 199, 215, 216.

CHAPTER 6

PHENOMENOLOGY APPLIED TO OTHER DISCIPLINES

Edmund Husserl not only saw phenomenology as a way of renewing traditional philosophic questions, he also conceived it to be a method applicable to the fundamental questions in every area of human inquiry. Whatever their other, peripheral disagreements might be, Husserl's successors in phenomenology agree that philosophy's task is to investigate the first principles assumed by each rational discipline, question its unfounded presuppositions, and show the limitations and scope of that discipline.

The application of the phenomenological method to other human disciplines is still in its beginning stages, but this is understandable. In its early period phenomenology had to devote much of its attention to an articulation and clarification of its own method, but its intention was always to provide the foundations for all areas of rational inquiry. A discussion of the variety of ways it has worked out in practice would require a treatment much longer than the limits of the present work allow. But a general introduction to the ways the phenomenological method is applied to other disciplines will show the many possibilities for the broadening of the role of philosophy in relation to other areas of investigation. In the following discussion, one or two paradigm cases in each area are briefly mentioned as an example of how phenomenology has been applied to various disciplines, and the selected bibliography refers to other efforts within the same field.

PHENOMENOLOGY
AND PSYCHOLOGY

At its very beginnings phenomenology was faced with the problem of the relationship between psychology and logic. It was Husserl's critique of the psychologistic interpretation of logic (that is, the view that logic can be explained in terms of empirical, psychic processes) that led him to phenomenology as a basic method for dealing with areas of human experience which are nonpsychological in the traditional sense. Central to Husserl's work, as has already been mentioned in previous chapters, was the discovery of the noetic-noematic structure of human consciousness. That is, every conscious activity can be analyzed in terms of its orientation and direction (noetic) and the objective correlate (noematic) toward which the noetic activity points. But these two poles of any conscious experience cannot be separated; one can be understood only in terms of the other, and neither has temporal priority.

Phenomenology is critical of traditional psychology for focusing on only the noematic dimension of experience and for interpreting the noetic in a materialistic sense. By basing its approach on a method borrowed from natural science, traditional psychology could not help but be concerned only with the observable and measurable aspects of human behavior. The cause and effect model became the explanation of all human activity; mental processes were reduced to empirical phenomena observable within a causal chain. It was only a short step to determinism, which claims that all mental phenomena are explainable in terms of reactions to prior stimuli and that the relationship between different mental events is mechanistic. This is another instance of the "nothing but" approach to psychology: thoughts are "nothing but" displacements in the brain of material particles; consciousness is "nothing but" the sum of these displacements; and all mental activity is "nothing but" the functioning of a highly complex mechanism reacting to its environment.

All this is antithetical to phenomenology for the reason that it leaves out the noetic structures of consciousness and their nonmaterial noematic correlates. In short, phenomenology charges that mechanistic psychology omits the most important aspect of human behavior, namely, its meaning. And in so doing it reduces itself to a subjectivistic contradiction: if all mental processes are *caused* by physical events, then the explanations of behavioral psychology are likewise *caused* by physical conditions and therefore have no universal validity. And yet by making the claim that all human behavior is "nothing but" the results of physical processes and reactions to an environment, behaviorism is making a claim to the universal validity of its explanations. If behavioral psychologists eliminate the meaning of mental activity from their area of investigation, they cannot then claim that their explanations have any meaning. But it is precisely the meaning of psychic events that phenomenology investigates.

The noetic dimension of any mental process is, in fact, the meaning of that process understood intentionally; that is, consciousness is always directed toward something, it can be a material object in some cases, or a nonmaterial object in other instances. This *object,* which is the correlate of any conscious activity, is the noematic dimension of consciousness, and traditional psychology (because of its methodological presuppositions) was not equipped to deal with it. The importance of the intentionality of consciousness in the phenomenological method has already been discussed *(see* pp. 8–9), and it should be clear how it becomes of primary importance for phenomenological psychology. Although it was excluded by traditional psychology, the meaning of conscious activity is the primary area of investigation for phenomenology.

What is the meaning, or the noetic dimension, of human activity? According to phenomenology it is the conscious orientation of all mental processes. For example, a person with a serious physical disability may orient himself toward the world in a way that leads him to despair and hopelessness. Another individual, with the same disability, may orient himself in a way that presents a challenge to be overcome, leading through optimism and courage to a meaningful life. This example points up the fact that the meaning of human activity cannot be accounted for solely in terms of physical characteristics. This is not to say that phenomenological psychology is not experimental; indeed it insists upon understanding all empirical aspects of behavior as important ingredients in the full understanding of human activity. But it rejects the claim that an empirical description of behavior is adequate as a total account of human action.

Although not known principally for his psychological studies, Martin Heidegger's influence has also been important in the development of phenomenological psychology. Heidegger's influence in psychology is, in a sense, an unplanned one, yet the themes with which Heidegger deals are broad, and psychology and other human sciences made ready use of them. Such human experiences as fear, anxiety, care, being-toward-death, time, and authentic-inauthentic situatedness were of interest to psychology, although it must be emphasized that Heidegger's ontological insights cannot be dissociated from ontic and psychological life. It takes only an alteration in attitude to make the psychological aspects obvious. By dealing with such themes as Being and being-in-the-world, Heidegger places man and his psyche in a context which psychology had never before considered. He has shown that a real understanding of man, be it normal or abnormal, is possible only by seeing him in relation to his world context.

Heidegger also had an effect on phenomenological psychology through his influence on Ludwig Binswanger (*see* no. 259). By adopting the notion of *Dasein* as being-in-the world which constitutes a relationship to an entire world prior to relationships with particular things, Binswanger rejects the notion of a sterile confrontation between subject and object. The world and self are correlative, and *Dasein* moves in the world in a multitude of ways. A real understanding of a person cannot be obtained by studying his organism or psyche; one has to study the person's world. Binswanger also employs such Heideggerian notions as spatiality and temporality. In terms of spatiality, one studies how, in our projection of ourselves in a world, we assign proper room for things in our space and how other spaces intersect each other. Esthetic space, the oriented space of movement, and natural space with its moods and the narrowed space of dread are all aspects of our spatiality. Temporality, as self-projection in the world, also has a multitude of psychological manifestations. The dream world may show an unattainable future, or fixation with parents; a tomb may show an inauthentic past in which nothing new can happen and which brings in its wake a disintegration of time at the present. For example, in melancholia the constitution of the world is loosened in such a way that suffering and guilt take control. Here self-reproach is based on the reversal of time. The future is extended to the past ("If only I had . . ."). Such spatial themes in dreams as climbing a mountain and losing one's way show the patient as having gotten himself into a position from which he can no longer extricate himself. Here one finds a discrepancy between the height of the goals aspired to and the capacities one has to reach them.

In addition to Heidegger and Binswanger, the work of Viktor Frankl in Europe and Rollo May in the United States is thoroughly phenomenological. And although they were not known primarily for their psychological analyses, Jean-Paul Sartre and Maurice Merleau-Ponty also contributed to the development of phenomenological psychology. To indicate how phenomenological psychology is applied to clinical situations, the work of Viktor Frankl will serve as a fruitful paradigm, for Frankl is not only a theoretician but has applied his phenomenological insights to specific clinical situations.

The most crucial period in Frankl's life was the five years he spent in concentration camps during the Second World War, and out of these experiences came his understanding of how phenomenological principles can be applied to the ultimate human crises. Frankl is now the recognized leader of a new movement in psychology and psychiatry, known variously as the new Vienna school or the "third force" in psychiatry (the first two being Freud and Jung). The basic method of analysis in Frankl's system is logotherapy, which reflects his view that the most basic problems in human behavior are questions of meaning (*logos* being the Greek word for "word" or "reason" and in this context referring to the structure of meaningful experience). Frankl's conviction is that human activity cannot be fully accounted for in terms of such drives as pleasure, power, or self-realization, for pleasure is the outcome of an activity that already has meaning for the individual, whereas power is not an end but a means towards the achievement of meaning. Neither can self-realization be the aim of human life, for self-realization is a side effect of actions directed toward meaning. In short, Frankl's view is that man's basic orientation is toward meaning, and life is a matter of choosing among various possible meanings.

Frankl's phenomenological orientation can be seen in his insistence that meaning cannot be reduced to psychological abstractions such as defense mechanisms or reaction formations. No person is willing to die for his defense mechanisms, but many persons are pushed to the brink (or over the brink) of self-destruction because they have been convinced that life is meaningless. The task for the clinical psychologist is to resort to the phenomenological analysis of immediate conscious experience and broaden for the patient his understanding of the noetic sphere of his experience, which reveals to him that life never ceases to have meaning. For Frankl, life is meaningful in a threefold way: (1) what one gives to life in terms of his unique and creative works; (2) what one takes from the world, namely, meanings and values which transcend the individual; and (3) the meaningful stance one takes with respect to those aspects of life which cannot be changed.

Against those who hold that the question of the meaning of life is not a proper one for psychology (or even that it is a meaningless question), Frankl claims that to avoid this question is to miss the very essence of what it means to be a human being. Indeed, central to Frankl's method is the insistence that the psychologist in a clinical situation must help the patient raise the question of the meaning of his life if he is to be of any help to the person. This grows out of Frankl's deep conviction that the basic conflicts in human experience are not "psychological" in the traditional sense (i.e., the result of suppressed drives, biological instincts, unconscious motivations) but originate in the noogenetic sphere (from the Greek word *noos*, "mind"). That is to say, such conflicts are the results of the collisions of values or meanings in man's search for the highest meaning in his life. The logotherapist sees his function as helping the patient discover this conflict for what it is and choose to orient himself in such a way that the conflict will be resolved. But the goal of the therapist is not a static balance among all values, for this is impossible; there will always remain a tension between what a man is at the present and the meaning which transcends the present and points toward what man ought to be. Frankl repeatedly quotes Goethe's lines: "if we take man as he is, we shall make him worse; only if we take him as he ought to be shall we make him better."

In the United States there is a growing awareness of phenomenological psychology, one indication being a series of conferences, the Lexington Conferences on Pure and Applied Phenomenology, organized by the Veterans Administration Hospital, Lexington, Kentucky. These conferences have explored topics ranging from questions of volition and action to specific pathological problems (*see* nos. 207, 237, 273, 274 for published lectures from these series). Although it by no means represents a majority point of view among psychologists in this country, phenomenological psychology has shown itself to be an alternative position that cannot be ignored.

PHENOMENOLOGY
AND RELIGION

Like all aspects of conscious activity, religious experience is also a valid area of phenomenological investigation. But the term *phenomenology of Religion* has been applied to the works of a variety of thinkers, many of whom have not explicitly used Husserl's phenomenological method in their analysis, although they may have employed a phenomenological approach broadly considered. Basic to the phenomenological investigation of religion is the description of the essence of religious experience as reflected in a variety of modes of expression. The work of Rudolf Otto *(The Idea of the Holy)*, Martin Buber *(I and Thou)*, Mircea Eliade *(The Sacred and the Profane)*, and Gerardus van der Leeuw *(Religion in Essence and Manifestation)* can thus be considered phenomenologies of religion in this broad sense. But for the purposes of the following discussion, attention will be directed to the work of philosophers who explicitly apply the phenomenological method to their investigation of religious experience.

The phenomenological approach to religion at the outset brackets all reductionistic theories that attempt to explain religion as nothing but the project of unfulfilled desires, the manifestations of a particular cultural milieu or a given historical situation, or as a subjectivistic response to uncontrollable forces. In other words, phenomenology takes as its point of departure the lived-experience of religion, attending not just to religious doctrines and beliefs but to the full range of religious phenomena—ritual, symbols and myths, cult, as well as religion's institutional manifestations. Whereas philosophy of religion, in its more traditional sense, was concerned mainly about the beliefs of various religions and attempted to understand and articulate their meaning and even to present arguments to justify their beliefs, the phenomenological approach is concerned with all experienced aspects of religion. Taking its data from both contemporary religions and the religions of antiquity, phenomenology seeks for the essence of the religious experience, by which is meant conscious experiencing and its objective correlate, while avoiding the assumption (popular among nineteenth-century philosophers) that all religions are simply particular manifestations of a universal religious consciousness. In this way phenomenology can attend to both the unity as well as diversity of different religious traditions.

An example of a phenomenological approach to one aspect of religious experience is the work of Paul Ricoeur, *The Symbolism of Evil* (*see* no. 290). This book is part of Ricoeur's larger *Philosophie de la volonté* (Philosophy of the Will) which includes an analysis of human volition (*see* no. 203) and an investigation into the structures of conscious experience that reveal fallibility as a possible but not a necessary result of the human situation (*see* no. 301). After these analyses, Ricoeur in *The Symbolism of Evil* turns to an investigation of man's conscious avowal of evil, which is always expressed at the most elementary level in symbols of stain, blot, or blemish, and which becomes "sin" when experienced in the presence of God. And when interiorized, these primary symbols are raised to the level of guilt. And finally, all these symbols are embodied in narratives, or myths, accounting for both the origin and the end of evil. Ricoeur focuses on four types of such myths: The Babylonian drama of creation myth, which views evil as a reversion to disorder and chaos; the Greek tragic myths, which view evil as the product of fate or divine caprice; the Adamic myth, which sees evil as the result of man's fall from a state of innocence; and the Orphic myth of the exiled soul, in which man is viewed as a soul-body duality and the body is looked on as the source as well as the occasion for evil. By examining these four types of myths in their dynamic interplay, Ricoeur attempts to develop a hermeneutic, or principle of interpretation, whereby these mythical expressions of consciousness of evil can be incorporated into rigorous philosophical reflection.

Phenomenology's greatest impact upon contemporary religious studies, however, has been through existential phenomenology, especially in the work of Martin Heidegger. Although Heidegger has written nothing on religion as such, his analyses in *Being and Time* (*see* no. 249) have been appropriated as a vehicle for the expression of New Testament doctrine by the work of Rudolf Bultmann, a New Testament scholar of considerable stature. Insisting that the world view of the New Testament differs radically from the scientific world view of contemporary, scientific man, Bultmann argues that the kerygma, or essential message of the New Testament, must be stripped of its mythical elements and communicated afresh to modern man in existentialist terms. This demythologization can be accomplished, Bultmann claims, by appropriating the analysis of the human situation articulated by Heidegger, which Bultmann finds to be a precise analogue to the Christian view of man. He notes that "Heidegger's existentialist analysis of the ontological structure of being would seem to be no more than a secularized, philosophical version of the New Testament view of human life."[1]

Bultmann's proposal to demythologize the message of the New Testament in order to restate it in existentialist categories created a considerable stir among theologians in the 1950s and 1960s and generated a vast literature both supporting and rejecting his project. Although demythologizing was the most controversial aspect of Bultmann's work, his major effort has been in the area of biblical scholarship, and his two-volume *Theology of the New Testament* has become a recognized work in New Testament scholarship, admired even by those who reject his more radical views.

An entire theology, more philosophical than biblical in orientation and unlike Bultmann's work in this respect, was developed by Paul Tillich. His massive three-volume *Systematic Theology* is one of the major works of philosophical theology of contemporary times and reflects an existentialist understanding of the human situation. Echoing themes from Kierkegaard and Dostoyevsky, as well as from contemporary philosophers, Tillich has provided an existentialist analysis of such major religious themes as the meaning of faith as existential choice, the significance of God as lying beyond the attempts to prove his existence objectively, and salvation as a new self-understanding which can best be characterized as the "new being." Although Tillich worked from the context of a Protestant, Christian heritage, existentialist theologies are by no means limited to a single religious tradition. The work of the Jewish theologian Martin Buber, the Catholic philosophers Gabriel Marcel and Jacques Maritain, and the Eastern Orthodox thinker Nicholas Berdyaev, are also cited as representative of existential theologies.

Although such diverse thinkers reflect different emphases, making gen-

1. Bultmann, "New Testament and Mythology," in *Kerygma and Myth*, edited by Bartsch, p. 24. *See* no. 279.

eralizations difficult, several summary statements can point to some of the central themes of existentialist theology. Accepting the phenomenological emphasis on human freedom, existential theology insists upon faith as free choice (echoing Kierkegaard's description of faith as a leap). Also in line with the phenomenological view of man, existential theology refuses to interpret human reality in merely objective terms and insists upon understanding man in his lived-situation. Dread, care, anguish, doubt, guilt, and ultimate commitment become significant foci for man's self-understanding. And in stressing the self-transcending dimension of human activity, existentialist theologians argue that man's authentic existence must be rooted in transcendence. (See page 38 for a discussion of transcendence.)

It would be accurate to say that the phenomenological investigation of religious experience, although already productive of several major works, is still in its beginning stages. But as the widespread interest in existential theology has demonstrated, the application of the phenomenological method—whether conceived in its broadest sense or in the narrower sense of a rigorous philosophical discipline, has already demonstrated its ability to shed new light on one of the most venerable human enterprises.

PHENOMENOLOGY AND
THE SOCIAL SCIENCES

Phenomenology does not limit the term "social sciences" only to the study of the structures of society but includes all areas of human life— education, literature, business and economics, history, as well as anthropology and sociology. In all these areas of inquiry, phenomenology's method of approach is rooted in the notion of the lived-world, previously discussed in chapter 3 (see pp. 45–47). The social world is primarily the lived-world as understood by common sense. Thus, we act in the world rather than observe it as disinterested scientists, and in the lived-world questions of epistemology, ontology, or the meaning of the world do not arise. In fact, they cannot even be admitted since they are not recognized as part of the lived-world.

Within the lived-world the reality of the world is never called into question, neither is any theoretical foundation given for it. Daily life is *ours* from the outset in that all elements of the world are taken as real for you as well as for me. The real is not based on empirical or logical inference or a predicative judgment but on a prepredicative understanding of the world. Therefore the social sciences, phenomenologically considered, deal not with the question of the reality of the world but rather with human relationships within this world. Thus, intersubjective relations and the question of knowledge of the other person are of primary importance for phenomenology. Husserl dealt with them at length in *Cartesian Meditations (see* no. 24), where he initiated a series of investigations of our knowledge of other persons and showed that, try as we may to avoid the assumption of our knowledge of other persons, we always find ourselves having this knowledge. For Husserl this meant that the world is never perceived as *mine* only but always as *ours.* We see our fellowman not theoretically but as someone, rather than something, and as someone like us. When encountering another individual, I encounter a person without having to go through the process of drawing an inference based on anatomical details that would allow me to classify him as a member of the human species. All this is accomplished on a pretheoretical level without the need of any rigorous demonstrations of the reality of the other. Alfred Schutz, one of the leading social phenomenologists, called this a "thou orientation." From the moment that I encounter the other, I am thou oriented, not in terms of a theoretical judgment but in an immediate lived-experience.

For Schutz, the social world is based on intersubjectivity in a number of ways. It is the area of my encounter of the other; it is the place where I perform all my acts directed toward objects, tasks, and others in the world; and my actions open up a world that is *ours* just as it is *mine.* In other words, I encounter the other person always in a context which does not depend upon his or my birth; it is a context historically based and existing before our birth and after our death. By *historically based,* Schutz does not mean a chronological succession of events *(Historie)* but history as lived in terms of moral codes, economic situations, religious practices —in short, *Geschichte.* Objects in the world exhibit this *Geschichte* as the imprint of others of previous generations. The imprint is not merely a material sign to which we react but a system of meanings which constitute the context in which we live. Language, religion, art, education, philosophy—in short, all cultural structures are manifestations of previous generations.

But not only is the lived-world open to the past in the way just mentioned, it is also open to the future which is partially *ours* but to a greater extent is also *theirs*—those who belong to future generations. The intersubjective world thus constitutes a temporal context for human actions open in both directions and contains systems of meaning for the individual within which he understands himself, things, and other persons. The intersubjective lived-world is the basic context of human action, and the work of Schutz is concerned with elucidating the meaning of actions within this context. Human actions must be understood, according to Schutz, in terms of their temporal directions and their accompanying intentional structures. The meaning of an action is bound up with these temporal distinctions but with the full understanding that the meaning is not added to the action but constitutes its very essence.

The phenomenological basis for social understanding permits the interpretation of human life in terms of goals, purposes, and meaning orientation. For example, labor can be analyzed phenomenologically in terms of the goals toward which it is oriented rather than as merely a reaction to the economic structures of society. As Max Scheler has pointed out, human labor is not simply a response to environmental conditions but is based on value orientation; what labor means to the laborer determines his attitude toward it. This can be seen clearly in societies in which material prosperity is not valued as a good; here labor is not understood as a means to acquiring physical comfort. In contrast, most Western societies have valued productivity as both an economic and social good. Hence, labor has taken on a meaning reflecting these values, and labor is seen as the means whereby an individual increases his collection of goods for the increased comfort of his family and himself.[2] Labor, although a process related to material conditions, cannot be reduced to these conditions, for values and goals play a role in labor that are irreducible to surrounding material conditions. The laborer cannot avoid the values of the past, neither can he avoid considerations concerning his expectations and hopes for himself and for future generations.

Like labor, education is also temporally oriented; it is always in a context of already given values and goals which constitute a tradition. Yet it is also for the sake of the future, not in terms of a private intention but an intention imprinted in the educational institutions themselves. Phenomenologically considered, education is more than the simple teaching and learning of particular reactions or a conditioning which would yield proper reaction formations. Nor is education a simple problem-solving process; it is rather necessary to understand the values on which educational institutions are based. Without an understanding of its traditional footing, education accepts this tradition uncritically and is incapable of any genuine newness in the future. If education is understood as a process of training technicians for an industrialized society, without understanding the basic values of that society, the outcome may be tragic in that the technicians will be incapable of evaluating those traditions in light of society's movement toward the future.

True to its method, phenomenology views society as comprising free

2. The work of the sociologist Max Weber, who is frequently quoted by Schutz, points up the importance of value systems in understanding the meaning of labor in a given society. A case in point is the value attributed to work in the Protestant ethic, which Weber sees as a contributing factor in the development of industrialized economy. *See* his *The Protestant Ethic and the Spirit of Capitalism*, translated by Talcott Parsons (New York: Scribner, 1958).

persons making choices within the context of the value system of the society. It sees the structures and institutions of society not as the product of material conditions or deterministic forces but the outcome of value considerations. Hence, to understand the structures of any society, it is necessary to understand the values which gave rise to the directions, goals, and meaning of these structures. One may change the material aspects of society's institutions, but if the values are not changed, the institutions remain the same. Or one may retain the material aspects of society's institutions while changing the values upon which they are based, with the result that one will experience them as different institutions. A case in point is when royal palaces are made into museums. In short, phenomenology insists upon openness to the full range of social reality, including the various levels of social objectivity, which includes values, goals, and meaning, as well as material objects.

PHENOMENOLOGY AND
THE NATURAL SCIENCES

Phenomenology originated within the controversy surrounding the question of the foundations of human knowledge and the role played by logic in rational thought, which led phenomenology to be more concerned with the human sciences than with the natural sciences. This kind of division, however, is not absolute, for both areas of investigation share a concern for an orderly investigation of reality. In English, however, *science* tends to connote only physical or natural science, whereas in German *Wissenschaft* includes both the natural sciences and the humanities, for *Wissenschaft* refers to any organized body of systematic knowledge. It is certainly the case that Husserl saw phenomenology's task as providing the rational basis for all sciences in the above sense, and it was a method applicable to the understanding and elucidation of the principles and axioms of natural science no less than the human sciences. For Husserl this was a cardinal notion inasmuch as he was convinced that no science—be it natural or humanistic—could derive its own principles from the scientific area it investigates. No science, for example, can prove its own assumptions scientifically. A physicist cannot prove scientifically the notion of cause and effect (as David Hume decisively pointed out), for this is a principle assumed a priori by his scientific procedure. Neither can a natural scientist prove scientifically that his activity is based on rational principles, for whenever a scientist reflects on the first principles of his science, he is no longer engaged in scientific but in philosophical inquiry.

Since all natural sciences assume the validity of logic and its principles of rational thought, any threat to the truth of logic is a threat to the very basis of science itself. Husserl showed that the psychologistic interpretation of logic is precisely such a threat, for if the principles of logic can be reduced to principles of psychology (as the psychologistic interpretation claimed) then science would lose its universal validity. All truth claims would be meaningless if indeed the "laws" of logic were only empirical generalizations of the way the human psyche just happened to function. Husserl's repudiation of psychologism has already been discussed (see chapter 2, pp. 17–21), but it is mentioned here again in order to point out that one of phenomenology's earliest efforts was directed toward a problem lying at the very foundation of all scientific endeavor.

Even though phenomenology's criticism of the unfounded assumptions of natural science may lead one to think that phenomenology is anti-scientific, the case is quite the contrary. In fact, phenomenology sees its task as twofold: (1) to show the basis for natural science in terms of justifying science's first principles and axioms, and (2) to show the limitations of the scientific method of investigation by placing it in the proper perspective. If the method of the natural sciences is incapable of dealing with values, consciousness, and meaning, as well as its own first principles, then it should relinquish these tasks to philosophy. Thus, phenomenology does not intend to preempt the tasks of the individual sciences, such as physics, chemistry, or biology. Phenomenology is not interested in compiling new data based on empirical research; this is the legitimate area for each particular science. Rather, it is phenomenology's task to clarify, justify, and delimit the first principles and the limits of the area of objectivity with which each particular science can deal.

A popular view of science is that it is a neutral method of observation and analysis, but philosophy shows that there is more involved than that. Before scientific observation can begin, there must already be present a theory which orients and directs this observation by including certain spheres of objectivity and excluding others. A particular object, such as a tree, does not demonstrate which area of its objectivity is the proper concern of physics, which parts are the area of investigation for chemistry, and which aspects are in the sphere of biology. Yet these distinctions are made by scientists, and they are made on the basis of assumptions which are not themselves scientific. Moreover, each special science assumes the unity of its object of investigation: for example, the assumption that the object persists through time, is identical with itself, and through its causal relation to other objects undergoes change. But such notions as unity, identity, change, and causality cannot be dealt with scientifically but are rather assumed in all scientific endeavors. Hence what constitutes unity, identity, and so forth is the proper area of philosophical investigation.

Even more basic is the assumption of values. Scientific activity is not performed merely because of the development of a scientific method but because a value has been placed upon science. Science, however, is not capable of investigating through its own methods the value of science and its application. Hence, science has developed techniques which have given rise to value controversies with which the natural sciences cannot deal. For example, genetic engineering, organ transplants, experimentation with human subjects, cloning, and a host of other techniques are within the range of scientific possibility but have raised questions which can only be answered on the basis of a value theory. The science of biology can describe the development of a fetus, tracing its origin from a single cell through its various stages of growth, but biology cannot answer the question of when the fetus becomes a human being. This is a question having philosophical and religious implications not answerable by the scientific method. Although a scientist might assume that additional and more sophisticated methods of observation might yield the answer sought for, it is phenomenology's claim that, in principle, such answers cannot be given by the scientific method.

The task of phenomenology, as Husserl conceived it, is to show the levels of objectivity assumed by any particular science—values, a priori theoretical principles, methods of investigation, and assumptions about the nature of reality. And by showing that all levels of objectivity are not amenable to the methods of the natural sciences, phenomenology guards against naive scientism, the narrowing of the range of investigation open to rational inquiry, and the application of the scientific method to inappropriate areas. All of these concerns were expressed in one of Husserl's late works, *The Crisis of European Sciences and Transcendental Phenomenology*. But Husserl had no intention of instituting a new dogmatism which would be just as tyrannical as the old. The spirit he brought to his criticism of the sciences was the Greek ideal of philosophy as the pursuit of wisdom and a love of truth, with the accompanying awareness of the infinite task that this entails.

> I seek not to instruct but only to lead, to point out and describe what I see. I claim no other right than that of speaking according to my best lights, principally before myself but in the same manner also before others, as one who has lived in all its seriousness the fate of a philosophical existence.[3]

---

3. Husserl, *The Crisis of European Sciences*, p. 18. *See* no. 25.

BIBLIOGRAPHY

*Phenomenology and
Psychology*

The significance of the application of phenomenological methods to psychology is shown by the existence of two journals devoted to exploring and developing this new approach to psychology. The journal *Human Inquiries* (originally titled *Review of Existential Psychology and Psychiatry*) is edited by Leslie Schaffer and published by the Association of Existential Psychology and Psychiatry. Another journal, entitled *Existential Psychiatry* (formerly called *Journal of Existential Psychiatry*), is published by the American Ontoanalytic Association and is edited by Jordan Scher. It also incorporates and continues the *Journal of Existentialism,* which is no longer a separate publication.

259. Binswanger, Ludwig. *Being in the World: Selected Papers of Ludwig Binswanger.* Translated by Jacob Needleman. New York: Basic Books, 1963.
     A critique of behaviorism showing its contradictions and analyzing psychic problems in terms of man and world.

260. Drüe, Herman. *Edmund Husserls System der phänomenologischen Psychologie.* Berlin: Walter de Gruyter, 1963.
     Excellent discussion of the problem posed to psychology by Cartesian dualism with a critique of Cartesianism, psychologism, and an analysis of the phenomenological method in application to psychology; extensive bibliography.

261. Frankl, Viktor E. *The Doctor and the Soul.* New York: Bantam, 1967.
     Critque of Freudian assumptions showing their inadequacies and offering as an alternative the basic outlines of logotherapy.

262. ———. *Man's Search for Meaning: An Introduction to Logotherapy.* New York: Washington Square Pr., 1969.
     Delineates the basic level of human constitution with which logotherapy deals, showing that man is not ruled by will to power or pleasure but will to meaning.

263. Goldstein, Kurt. *Selected Papers.* Edited by Aron Gurwitsch et al. The Hague: Martinus Nijhoff, 1970.
     Shows the necessity of different attitudes such as concrete and abstract for a full understanding of some psychic phenomena.

264. Kockelmans, Joseph J. *Edmund Husserl's Phenomenological Psychology: A Historico-Critical Study.* Pittsburgh: Duquesne Univ. Pr., 1967.

265. Koestenbaum, Peter. *The Vitality of Death: Essays in Existential Psychology and Philosophy.* Westport, Conn.: Greenwood, 1971.
Shows how the differing attitudes toward death shape human action and world views.

266. May, Rollo. *Existential Psychology.* Rev. ed. New York: Random, 1969.
Discusses the existential approach to psychology in its clinical applications.

267. Minkowski, Eugène. *Lived Time: Phenomenological and Psychopathological Studies.* Translated by Nancy Metzel. Evanston, Ill.: Northwestern Univ. Pr., 1933.
The author is a psychiatrist who shows, from his own clinical experience, that time and space are organized differently by the pathological consciousness.

268. Pleassner, Helmuth. *Laughing and Crying: A Study of the Limits of Human Behavior.* Translated by James S. Churchill and Marjorie Grene. Evanston, Ill.: Northwestern Univ. Pr., 1972.
An attempt to describe laughing and crying as uniquely human responses which reveal human nature in its limit situations.

269. Ricoeur, Paul. *Freud and Philosophy: On Interpretation.* Translated by Denis Savage. New Haven: Yale Univ. Pr., 1970.
Philosophical analysis of Freud showing areas of compatibility between psychoanalysis and phenomenology but criticizing Freudian psychology as an adequate view of man.

270. Spiegelberg, Herbert. *Phenomenology in Psychology and Psychiatry: A Historical Introduction.* Evanston, Ill.: Northwestern Univ. Pr., 1972.
Shows the uses of phenomenological method in psychology and psychiatry; gives a historical survey of the development of phenomenological psychology and discusses the major representatives of the movement. Good bibliography.

271. Straus, Erwin W. *Phenomenological Psychology: The Selected Papers of Erwin W. Straus.* Translated by Erling Eng. New York: Basic Books, 1966.
Deals with human structures of experience such as spatiality, movement, upright posture, human actions, and some clinical studies.

272. ———. *Psychologie der menschlichen Welt: Gesammelte Schriften.* Berlin: Springer Verlag, 1960.
Straus' collected writings on such topics as time experience in depressive persons, suggestions, expression, and inner freedom.

273. ———, and Griffith, Richard, eds. *Phenomenology of Memory: The Third Lexington Conference on Pure and Applied Phenomenology*. Pittsburgh: Duquesne Univ. Pr., 1970.

Leading phenomenologists and psychologists discuss memory and its relationship to psychic problems both from experimental and phenomenological perspectives.

274. ———, and ———, eds. *Phenomenology: Pure and Applied: The First Lexington Conference on Pure and Applied Phenomenology*. Pittsburgh: Duquesne Univ. Pr., 1964.

Papers read at the first Lexington Conference showing various ways phenomenology can be applied to clinical psychological situations.

275. ———; Natanson, Maurice; and Ey, Henri. *Psychiatry and Philosophy*. Translated by Erling Eng and Stephen C. Kennedy. New York: Springer, 1969.

Deals with basic phenomenological concepts as they relate to the psychiatric conception of normalcy.

276. Van Baeyer, Walter, and Griffith, Richard M., eds. *Conditio Humana: Erwin W. Straus on His 75th Birthday*. New York: Springer, 1966.

Leading phenomenologists and psychologists deal with such questions as psychological method, abnormal personality, motherhood, intentionality, and volition. Complete bibliography of Straus' works up to 1966.

277. Van den Berg, Jan Hendrick. *The Changing Nature of Man: Introduction to a Historical Psychology, Metabletica*. Translated by H. F. Croes. New York: Norton, 1961.

Deals with Cartesian dualism in psychology and investigates basic human relationships such as those of adults and children, man and society, from an existential perspective.

278. Van Kamm, Adrian. *Existential Foundations of Psychology*. Pittsburgh: Duquesne Univ. Pr., 1966.

Deals with the nature of science as a mode of being-in-the-world and explicates the phenomenological method, showing its application to psychology.

Also see nos. 16, 20, 70, 94, 102, 197.

Phenomenology
and Religion

The following selected bibliography indicates only a few of the major works showing the relationship between phenomenology or existential-phenomenology and theological studies. There is a vast literature on the subject, including numerous secondary works on major figures such as Bultmann and Tillich, as well as many efforts at applying existential themes to theology. Also cited are works of thinkers who can only be considered phenomenological in the broad sense, but these are important in showing how widely the term *phenomenology* has been applied in religious studies.

279. Bartsch, Hans Werner, ed. *Kerygma and Myth: A Theological Debate.* Translated by Reginald H. Fuller. London: S.P.C.K., 1960.
    Contains Bultmann's original proposal concerning the use of Heideggerian analysis in demythologizing the New Testament kerygma and a collection of responses to Bultmann.

280. ———, ed. *Kerygma and Myth: A Theological Debate,* vol. 2. Translated by Reginald H. Fuller. London: S.P.C.K., 1962.
    Continuation of the above, with Bultmann's reply to Karl Jaspers' criticism of demythologizing.

281. Bettis, Joseph Dabney, ed.. *Phenomenology of Religion: Eight Modern Descriptions of the Essence of Religion.* New York: Harper & Row, 1969.
    The editor's introduction explains the various senses in which the term *phenomenology of religion* has been used, and the selections in the book reflect an understanding of phenomenology in the broad sense. Excerpts include selections from Merleau-Ponty, van der Leeuw, Maritain, Tillich, Eliade, Buber, and others.

282. Buber, Martin. *I and Thou.* 2d ed. Translated by Ronald Gregor Smith. New York: Scribner, 1958.
    Rejects attempts to understand God as an object of thought and argues that the divine is the Eternal Thou mirrored in all lesser genuine I-Thou relationships.

283. Buri, Fritz. *Theology of Existence.* Greenwood, S.C.: Attic Pr., 1965.
    Contribution by a post-Bultmannian who considers Bultmann's demythologizing not radical enough.

284. Earle, William; Edie, James M.; and Wild, John. *Christianity and Existentialism.* Evanston, Ill.: Northwestern Univ. Pr., 1963.
    Analysis of the existential themes of choice, decision, and absurdity as they relate to Christian theology both in its historical roots and its contemporary expressions.

285. Eliade, Mircea. *The Sacred and the Profane: The Nature of Religion.* Translated by Willard R. Trask. New York: Harcourt, Brace, 1959.
    Descriptive analysis of the essential nature of religion with reference to

the myths and rituals of primitive religions; not phenomenological in the strict sense.

286. Herberg, Will, ed. *Four Existentialist Theologians*. Garden City, N.Y.: Doubleday, Anchor, 1958.

Selections from the work of Jacques Maritain, Nicolas Berdyaev, Martin Buber, and Paul Tillich.

287. Luijpen, William A. *Phenomenology and Atheism*. Translated by Walter van de Putte. Pittsburgh: Duquesne Univ. Pr., 1964.

Discusses the atheism of Marx, Nietzsche, Sartre, and Merleau-Ponty but argues that existential phenomenology is not inherently atheistic.

288. Macquarrie, John. *An Existentialist Theology: A Comparison of Heidegger and Bultmann*. London: SCM Pr., 1955.

Definitive analysis of Bultmann's adaptation of Heideggerian philosophy suggesting the limitations of an existentialist interpretation of the New Testament.

289. Otto, Rudolf. *The Idea of the Holy*. Translated by John W. Harvey. 2d ed. London: Oxford Univ. Pr., 1950.

Analysis of the object of religious experience as the *mysterium tremendum* or Wholly Other, which gives rise to the experience of the numinous or the "holy."

290. Ricoeur, Paul. *The Symbolism of Evil*. Translated by Emerson Buchanan. New York: Harper & Row, 1967.

Analysis of the symbols and myths which are the vehicle for expression of conscious experience of evil. Translation of the second part of volume 2 of Ricoeur's *Philosophie de la volonté*.

291. Tillich, Paul. *The Courage to Be*. New Haven: Yale Univ. Pr., 1952.

Shows that courage in the face of such experiences as anxiety, despair, and guilt can only give rise to faith when it is rooted in transcendence.

292. ———. *Systematic Theology*. 3 vols. Chicago: Univ. of Chicago Pr., 1951–63.

Most complete statement of Tillich's theology, which reflects an existentialist analysis of the meaning of religous experience.

293. Van der Leeuw, Gerardus. *Religion in Essence and Manifestation: A Study in Phenomenology*. Translated by J. E. Turner. London: Allen & Unwin, 1938.

First published in German in 1933, this descriptive study applies the Husserlian notion of the epoche in a very broad sense and offers an account of the subjective nature of religious experience and its objective correlates.

Also see no. 372.

Phenomenology and the
Social Sciences

Because phenomenology sees its task as investigating the foundations of humanistic disciplines, many works defy neat classification. The following are representative of work being done that relates to various social sciences; for the application of phenomenology to literature, *see* the bibliography on phenomenology and language in chapter 5 (pp. 115–16).

294. Chamberlin, John Gordon. *Toward a Phenomenology of Education*. Philadelphia: Westminister Pr., 1969.

   Deals with the various dimensions of human interaction in educational situations, such as moral rules, ideologies, relations to nature, esthetic preferences, and the functions of culture, institutions, and the teaching process itself.

295. Landgrebe, Ludwig. *Phänomenologie und Geschichte*. Gütersloh: Gütersloher Verlaghaus, 1968.

   Deals with the problems of history in transcendental phenomenology, life-philosophies, and dialectics.

296. Merleau-Ponty, Maurice. *Humanism and Terror: An Essay on the Communist Problem*. Translated by John O'Neill. Boston: Beacon, 1969.

   Discussion of the social theories of Marxism as exemplified in the Soviet Union, warning against the dangers of dogmatism and the temptation of making dialectic into an explicit method.

297. Miller, Albert J. *Selective Bibliography of Existentialism in Education and Related Topics*. Jericho, N.Y.: Exposition, 1969.

298. Natanson, Maurice. *Literature, Philosophy, and the Social Sciences: Essays in Existentialism and Phenomenology*. The Hague: Martinus Nijhoff, 1962.

   Presents the philosophical foundations of phenomenology and applies them in the investigation of fine arts, society, and history.

299. ———, ed. *Phenomenology and Social Reality: Essays in Memory of Alfred Schutz*. The Hague: Martinus Nijhoff, 1970.

300. Ranly, Ernest W. *Scheler's Phenomenology of Community*. The Hague: Martinus Nijhoff, 1966.

   Discusses the various levels of human relationships and bases them on respect for a love of persons.

301. Ricoeur, Paul. *Fallible Man*. Translated by Charles Kelbley. Chicago: Regnery, 1965.

Foundational studies leading toward a philosophical anthropology showing the self-transcendent movement implicit in knowing, acting, and feeling. Translation of the first part of volume 2 of *Philosophie de la volonté*.

302. Schutz, Alfred. *On Phenomenology and Social Relations: Selected Writings*. Edited by Helmut B. Wagner. Chicago: Univ. of Chicago Pr., 1970.
    Indicates how Schutz applied phenomenological method in the investigation of all aspects of social reality, their levels of objectivity, and modes of relatedness. Good bibliography.

303. Strasser, Stephan. *The Idea of Dialogical Phenomenology*. Pittsburgh: Duquesne Univ. Pr., 1969.
    Argues that phenomenology is an intersubjective enterprise; contains good bibliography.

304. Strasser, Stephan. *Phenomenology and the Human Sciences: A Contribution to a New Scientific Ideal*. Translated by John R. Kanda. Pittsburgh: Duquesne Univ. Pr., 1963.
    Critique of naturalism and positivism and argues for a broader methodology based on different levels of experience.

305. Vandenberg, Donald. *Being and Education: Essays in Existential Phenomenology*. Englewood Cliffs, N.J.: Prentice-Hall, 1971.
    Shows the role of philosophy in education, the sociohistorical context, values, and the truth of Being in intellectual encounter.

306. Wütenberger, Thomas, ed. *Phänomenologie, Rechtsphilosophie, Jurisprudenz: Festschrift für Gerhart Husserl*. Frankfort: Vittorio Klostermann Verlag, 1968.
    Authors in different disciplines deal with the influence and application of phenomenology in the areas of philosophy of law and jurisprudence.

Also see nos. 96, 97, 98, 125.

Phenomenology and the
Natural Sciences

Because phenomenology is concerned with the foundations of all rational endeavors, many phenomenological works dealing with the basis of logic and with questions of ontology are relevant to the discussion of the role of natural science. The following entries, however, give some indication of the specialized work that phenomenology is accomplishing in regard to individual disciplines within the natural sciences.

307. Ingarden, Roman. *Der Streit um die Existenz der Welt.* 3 vols. Tübingen: Max Niemeyer Verlag, 1964–65.

A student of Husserl, Ingarden applies phenomenological method in order to distinguish different scientific regions, which he insists must have an ontological foundation.

308. Jonas, Hans. *The Phenomenon of Life: Toward a Philosophical Biology.* New York: Harper & Row, 1966.

Deals with Darwinism, the range and limits of quantitative methodology, and the question of purpose in life-processes.

309. Kockelmans, Joseph J. *Phenomenology and Physical Science: An Introduction to the Philosophy of Physical Science.* Pittsburgh: Duquesne Univ. Pr., 1966.

An introduction to the phenomenological concept of natural science and a delineation of its area of investigation.

310. ———, and Kisiel, Theodore, eds. *Phenomenology and the Natural Sciences.* Evanston, Ill.: Northwestern Univ. Pr., 1970.

An anthology of articles, some of which originally were published in Europe, dealing with the contributions made by phenomenologists to the natural sciences.

311. Tymieniecka, Anna-Teresa. *Phenomenology and Science in Contemporary European Thought.* New York: Farrar, Straus, & Cudahy, 1962.

Deals with the required phenomenological foundations of a number of sciences showing the techniques of investigation and the progress already made.

312. Van Melsen, Andrew G. *Science and Technology.* Pittsburgh: Duquesne Univ. Pr., 1961.

Deals with the nature of physical science, its operations and assumptions, and shows some of the historical developments of the concept of nature and technology.

CHAPTER 7

THE
ONGOING
TASKS
OF
PHENOMENOLOGY

This study has shown the wide diversity of viewpoints, subject areas, and variations of method, all of which nevertheless have contributed to the development of phenomenology. It should now be obvious that phenomenology is not a homogeneous and dogmatic philosophy but a way of reopening the basic philosophic issues that deal with the foundational questions of all human endeavors. As phenomenology becomes a more widely practiced method of philosophy, the danger is that it will be understood as a philosophy in itself. Something of the sort has happened to linguistic analysis, which originated as a method of approaching philosophical questions but has taken on the status of an independent philosophy. Method in itself, as Whitehead has pointed out, is merely a neutral tool for philosophy and should never be identified with philosophy. And the previous survey of phenomenology has made apparent that there is no *one* single phenomenological method but rather a broad spectrum of ways of approaching traditional philosophic problems. The phenomenological method, however, can be distinguished from alternative approaches, but it is impossible to formalize it into a rigid system. In fact, the extent to which phenomenology's method can be formalized at all depends on the subject area under investigation.

No better example can be found than Husserl himself, who constantly reexamined and rethought the question of method. It should, therefore, be no shock to discover that Husserl's successors are still concerned with a careful articulation of the phenomenological method. And neither should it be surprising to discover that there still remains disagreement among phenomenologists as to the precise limits of the phenomenological method. The usual resolution of this question, however, is not so much methodological as it is based on the concrete investigation of a given subject area. And although it is possible to distinguish between pure and applied phenomenology, this distinction is not absolute inasmuch as phenomenology has no genuine validity until it is applied—that is, until it is brought to bear on a specific area of investigation.

Pure phenomenology has a number of tasks, one of which is the elaboration of the phenomenological method, but always in view of a particular set of phenomena which are being analyzed. In other words, the researches of those engaged in *pure* phenomenology are always content-oriented. On the other hand, *applied* phenomenology does not need to dwell on method, since the process of investigation by way of the phenomenological method collapses into the content of the description being undertaken. Thus, the difference between *pure* and *applied* phenomenology is one of emphasis.

The fact that pure and applied phenomenology cannot ultimately be separated became obvious to Husserl. His attempt to articulate a pure, eidetic phenomenology involved him in problems which he could not resolve within the transcendental attitude. In order for transcendental phenomenology to be successful, Husserl noted that he had to assume too much—for example, the existence of other selves. In his attempt to account for the existence of other egos, Husserl discovered that he could not have a pure and presuppositionless point of departure; whenever he began to investigate the problems of intersubjectivity, he found himself assuming the existence of the phenomena he was attempting to analyze. And what is more, he discovered in the phenomena more than any transcendental analysis could exhaust. Consequently, Husserl was led to the conviction that no transcendental description could be either presuppositionless or exhaustive. But this conclusion became obvious to Husserl only after he had invested a great deal of effort in his attempt to articulate a pure, eidetic phenomenology. And, in fact, he may never have really abandoned the hope that such an eidetic phenomenology could be achieved.

This period of Husserl's work remains one of the most controversial aspects of his phenomenology. Had Husserl lived longer, perhaps he would have abandoned this project entirely, but one will, of course, never know. It is fair to say, however, that most contemporary phenomenologists—including existential phenomenologists—have abandoned it. They find that the language Husserl used in his articulation of eidetic phenomenology presupposed a kind of idealistic orientation which they found inconsistent with the way we experience the world. Whether or not Husserl's eidetic phenomenology was idealistic or not remains an ongoing controversy for specialists, but this issue does not detract from the contributions which Husserl made to the development of phenomenology.

Partially in response to the problems he encountered in his own work in eidetic phenomenology, and partially in response to the criticisms of his coworkers, Husserl's later work veered away from eidetic phenomenology to an analysis of the world of ordinary experience—the lived-world—which all his previous philosophical analysis had assumed. It led to an investigation of history and its meaning, which is presupposed by language, culture, and all valuational activities. Although Husserl's work on the lived-world provided the point of departure for existential phenomenology, the recognition of the primacy of the lived-world by existentialists was different from Husserl's investigation of it. Husserl's concern was to investigate the lived-world on the basis of conscious intentionality, whereas existential phenomenology begins with the notion of being-in-the-world, that is, being situated in the world in a context that is open to unlimited possibilities. Consequently, the existentialists' emphasis on such facets of experience as freedom of choice, embodiment, intersubjectivity, the meaning of existence, and the transcendent dimensions of experience, stress aspects of man's lived situation which Husserl did not investigate. This is not to say that existential philosophy is opposed to phenomenology as Husserl conceived it but rather that it explores the more concrete and immediate human concerns as they arise in lived-situations. One could suppose that Husserl would not have disagreed with this emphasis, but it is clear that his own concerns lay elsewhere. The development of existential phenomenology does, however, show that phenomenology's method is open to more variations than Husserl investigated.

As is true of any living discipline which has not yet rigidified into a formalism, phenomenology faces a number of unresolved issues. Not the least of these is the confusion in the minds of many persons as to the process of phenomenological analysis itself. Because of phenomenology's emphasis upon description as the primary task of philosophy, it is tempting to label any description as phenomenological. But this is most decidedly a distortion of the intent of phenomenology. Not just any description of experience is phenomenological, for basic to the phenomenological method is the exclusion of naturalistic assumptions about the ontological status of the world, including one's subjective reactions to it. Therefore, an ongoing task of phenomenology is constantly to clarify the naturalistic assumptions operative in description and to make apparent the experiential factors inherent in that description. Much published work that is labeled phenomenological does not employ phenomenological methods, and perhaps it is due, in part, to the lack of care with which phenomenologists have articulated their method. It is, therefore, an ongoing task of phenomenology to clarify its modes of procedure and their application to concrete areas of investigation.

Allied with this task is the difficulty, previously alluded to, of describing the nature of the phenomenological reduction. Due to the fact that philosophers working within the phenomenological tradition usually address each other in their published works, the danger is always present that a nonspecialist will understand phenomenology in terms of the naturalistic assumptions which it attempts to avoid. Effective communication with other philosophical viewpoints requires careful and open dialogue, else phenomenology faces the risk of becoming an arcane and inbred discipline. It would be unfortunate for phenomenology and in direct opposition to the intent of Husserl's work.

Discussions among phenomenologists themselves continue to focus on a number of unresolved issues. Basic to these discussions is the question of the extent to which various areas are open to phenomenological analysis and the limits that are necessary to such analysis. Perhaps the best example would be the question of ontology itself. Although many thinkers working within the phenomenological tradition have dealt with ontology (Heidegger, Merleau-Ponty, Landgrebe), each approaches the question of Being from a different perspective, and at least at this point none of these investigations has provided a satisfactory explication of Being. Perhaps the investigations of Heidegger's fundamental ontology represent the most extensive work in this area, yet Heidegger himself admits that his investigations into the question of Being are only a preliminary stage to future inquiries. And his cryptic suggestion that perhaps Being is not yet ready to reveal itself does not really resolve the difficulties of his ontology.

Although undertaken from a different perspective, the work of Merleau-Ponty encounters a similar difficulty. The "savage being" given in perception is never exhaustible in any set of descriptions but always leads further into an inexhaustible matrix of meanings. Ludwig Landgrebe's investigations show two possibilities: (1) that ontology might be approached by way of transcendental subjectivity as an assumed ontological background out of which the world is constituted; and (2) that ontology could proceed through the overcoming of the subject-object dichotomy by way of the lived-world.[1] For Landgrebe, the lived-world implies a nonexplicated belief in the substantiality of the world, and the task of ontology would be to explicate this belief, or what he calls the "doxic" aspects of lived-experience. All of these three approaches to ontology aim at the same problem, but which of them will become most predominant is for the future development of phenomenology to determine.

Another problem of continuing concern to phenomenology is the articulation of the various regions of conscious experience. In Husserl's transcendental phenomenology, the various regions of conscious experience are seen to be unified in the very structures of consciousness itself —and specifically the consciousness of time constitution. For existential phenomenology, which largely rejects the transcendental approach, the different regions of conscious experience are understood in terms of modes of being-in-the-world. But a problem faced by existential philosophy is that of accounting for the unity of these various regions. Jaspers attempted to account for it in terms of the Encompassing *(Das Umgreifende)* which, however, is never reached by consciousness but only pointed to by the various modes of consciousness. Heidegger's notion of Being is another attempt to account for this unity but, by his own admission, it has only a preliminary validity. Marcel's notion of the mystery of Being is a recognition of a deeper ontological unity than is given in experience, but by placing Being in the sphere of mystery, Marcel has put this unity beyond the scope of phenomenological analysis.

As was previously mentioned, Husserl attempted to find the unity of all regions of experience by way of transcendental time constitution. But this approach assumed that time can become an object of phenomenological investigation, a claim which Husserl's successors (specifically Eugen Fink and Merleau-Ponty) have shown to be illegitimate. Since every object and subject of experience is already in time, time itself can never be one among the other objects of experience and cannot be investigated as a noematic correlate of consciousness. Heidegger's approach to time is through an analysis of it as an always coming future possibility, which is the possibility of Being—hence the close identification of time *as* Being. But Heidegger's interpretation cannot account for the present unification of the modes of being-in-the-world. Heidegger's failure to give a clear statement concerning the unifying principle of being-in-the-world has given rise to a continuing controversy among interpreters of his work concerning which mode of being-in-the-world is primary. Some insist that care *(Sorge)* is primary, whereas others insist that time, being-toward-death, or openness is more fundamental. Until Heidegger clarifies

1. Ludwig Landgrebe, *Der Weg der Phänomenologie: Das Problem einer ursprünglichen Erfahrung* (Gütersloh: Gütersloher Verlagshaus, 1963). *See also* nos. 4, 251, and 295.

what he means by Being as time, such disagreements are likely to continue.

As phenomenology addresses itself to the foundational questions of the human sciences, it has come up against the fact that these other disciplines cannot be reduced to the principles of one philosophical system. What is needed is a bridge between phenomenology and the various methodologies of the human sciences—such as anthropology, sociology, psychology, history of religions, and so forth. Phenomenology, however, sees its task as providing an analysis of the basic assumptions lying behind the methods employed in these disciplines, but in order to accomplish this philosophy must first show the possible ways of interpreting these assumptions. These principles of interpretation constitute a method referred to as *hermeneutics* (from the Greek word for "interpretation"). Hermeneutics is an attempt to show the prephilosophical understanding of man in the world that is basic to these various disciplines so that this understanding can become the basis of philosophical reflection. Hermeneutics, therefore, has become a prominent aspect in the work of Heidegger, Gadamer, and Ricoeur. Heidegger's hermeneutics is concerned principally with an interpretation of Being. Gadamer is more concerned with the interpretation of language, and Ricoeur with the symbolisms implicit in religious experience and in psychoanalysis. Hermeneutics shows the multitude of expressions which point to a common understanding of meaning, movement, space, and time—as well as other aspects of human experience—which arise first on a prephilosophical level. Hermeneutics, however, is not external to phenomenological philosophy but rather shows the many possibilities of explicating a particular preunderstanding of a body of knowledge. For example, in esthetic criticism there is already a precritical understanding of the field of esthetics which allows the critic to understand what makes an artist artistic and what makes a particular object a work of art. These assumptions may not be explicit to either the artist or the critic, for it is not esthetics' task to explicate its own assumptions. But also basic to these presuppositions is an understanding of man which is tacitly assumed, the explication of which constitutes one interpretation of man's lived-situation. As an extension of the phenomenological method, hermeneutics constitutes a way of dealing with possible approaches to a subject matter. What is significant about hermeneutics is that it once again places philosophy in its traditional role of bringing to light the basic understandings implicit in all human endeavors.

This recapitulation of some of the controversial aspects of phenomenological philosophy, as well as the brief survey of several current concerns, demonstrates phenomenology's vitality in dealing with basic philosophical issues. And the range of interests reflected in phenomenological literature suggests that phenomenology has succeeded in broadening the scope of philosophy to encompass all human concerns. Whether it will retain this vitality or merely crystalize into another dogmatism remains to be seen. One would be foolish to make a prediction about phenomenology's prospects, for Hegel reminds us that philosophy should be silent about the future: the owl of Minerva, he notes, flies only at dusk.

**BIBLIOGRAPHIES
ON
INDIVIDUAL
PHILOSOPHERS**

The purpose of the following bibliographies is to orient the reader to the literature developed by individual philosophers who have contributed to the advancement of phenomenology and existential phenomenology. Where works by these thinkers have already been cited in chapter bibliographies, they will be referred to by cross references. The following listings are not exhaustive, but within the secondary sources cited are bibliographies which do offer fairly complete guides to the literature available on each thinker. Where published bibliographies exist, they have been included in the citations.

EXISTENTIAL BACKGROUNDS

Important for understanding the historical roots of existentialism is the work of two nineteenth-century philosophers—Søren Kierkegaard and Friedrich Nietzsche. A massive literature has been produced on both thinkers, and the following are only mentioned as representative works which will serve as introductions to their life and thought.

SØREN KIERKEGAARD
Primary Sources

313. *The Concept of Dread.* Translated by Walter Lowrie. Princeton, N.J.: Princeton Univ. Pr., 1957.

314. *The Concept of Irony, with Constant Reference to Socrates.* Translated by Lee M. Capel. New York: Harper & Row, 1966.

315. *Concluding Unscientific Postscript.* Translated by David F. Swenson and Walter Lowrie. Princeton, N.J.: Princeton Univ. Pr., 1941.

316. *Either/Or: A Fragment of Life.* Translated by David F. Swenson and Lillian Marvin Swenson. Princeton, N.J.: Princeton Univ. Pr., 1944.

317. *Fear and Trembling and The Sickness unto Death.* Translated by Walter Lowrie. Princeton, N.J.: Princeton Univ. Pr., 1968.

318. *Philosophical Fragments; or a Fragment of Philosophy, by Johannes Climacus.* Translated by David F. Swenson. Princeton, N.J.: Princeton Univ. Pr., 1936.

319. *Stages on Life's Way.* Translated by Walter Lowrie. London: Oxford Univ. Pr., 1940.

Secondary Sources

320. Lowrie, Walter. *Kierkegaard.* 2 vols. New York: Harper & Row, Harper Torchbooks, 1962.

321. Mackey, Louis. *Kierkegaard: A Kind of Poet.* Philadelphia: Univ. of Pennsylvania Pr., 1971.

322. Thompson, Josiah. *The Lonely Labyrinth: Kierkegaard's Pseudonymous Works.* Carbondale, Ill.: Southern Illinois Univ. Pr., 1967.

FRIEDRICH NIETZSCHE
Collected Works

323. *Complete Works.* 18 vols. Edited by Oscar Levy. 1909–11. Reprint. New York: Russell & Russell, 1964.

Secondary Sources

324. Jaspers, Karl. *Nietzsche: An Introduction to the Understanding of His*

Philosophical Activity. Translated by Charles F. Wallraff and Frederick J. Schmitz. Tucson: Univ. of Arizona Pr., 1965.

325. Kaufmann, Walter. *Nietzsche: Philosopher, Psychologist, Anti-Christ.* Princeton, N.J.: Princeton Univ. Pr., 1950.

326. Schlechta, Karl. *Der Fall Nietzsche: Aufträge und Vorsätze.* 2d ed. Munich: Carl Hanser Verlag, 1959.

NICHOLAS BERDYAEV
Primary Sources

327. *The Beginning and the End.* Translated by R. M. French. London: Geoffrey Bles, 1952.

328. *The Destiny of Man.* Translated by Natalie Duddington. New York: Harper & Row, 1960.

329. *The Divine and the Human.* Translated by R. M. French. London: Geoffrey Bles, 1949.

330. *Dream and Reality: An Essay in Autobiography.* Translated by Katherine Lambert. New York: Collier, 1962.

331. *The End of Our Time.* Translated by Donald Atwater. New York: Sheed & Ward, 1933.

332. *Fate of Man in the Modern World.* Translated by Donald A. Lowrie. Ann Arbor, Mich.: Univ. of Michigan Pr., 1961.

333. *The Meaning of History.* Translated by George Reavey. Cleveland: Meridian, 1962.

334. *The Meaning of the Creative Act.* Translated by Donald A. Lowrie. New York: Collier, 1962.

335. *Solitude and Society.* Translated by George Reavey. London: Geoffrey Bles, 1948.

336. *Spirit and Reality.* Translated by George Reavey. London: Geoffrey Bles, 1933.

337. *Truth and Revelation.* Translated by R. M. French. New York: Collier, 1962.

Also see *Freedom and Spirit* (no. 201) and *Slavery and Freedom* (no. 202).

Secondary Sources

338. Allen, Edgar. *Freedom in God: A Guide to the Thought of Nicolas Berdyaev*. New York: Philosophical Library, 1951.

339. Clarke, Oliver Fielding. *Introduction to Berdyaev*. London: Geoffrey Bles, 1950.

340. Richardson, David Bonner. *Berdyaev's Philosophy of History: An Existentialist Theory of Social Creativity and Eschatology*. The Hague: Martinus Nijhoff, 1968.

TWENTIETH-CENTURY EXISTENTIALISTS

MARTIN HEIDEGGER
Primary Sources

341. *Discourse on Thinking*. Translated by John M. Anderson and E. Hans Freund. New York: Harper & Row, Harper Torchbooks, 1966.

342. *Existence and Being*. Translated by D. Scott et al. Chicago: Regnery, 1949.

343. *Hegel's Concept of Experience*. Translated by Kenley Royce Dove. New York: Harper & Row, 1970.

344. "The Idea of Phenomenology." Translated by John N. Deely et al. *New Scholasticism* 44 (1970):325–44.

345. *Identity and Difference*. Translated by Joan Stambaugh. New York: Harper & Row, Harper Torchbooks, 1969.

346. *Kant and the Problem of Metaphysics*. Translated by James S. Churchill. Bloomington, Ind.: Indiana Univ. Pr., 1962.

347. *What Is a Thing?* Translated by W. B. Barton, Jr. and Vera Deutsch. Chicago: Regnery, 1968.

348. *What Is Called Thinking?* Translated by Fred D. Wick and J. Glenn Gray. New York: Harper & Row, Harper Torchbooks, 1970.

Also see *Being and Time* (no. 249), *An Introduction to Metaphysics* (no. 250), *On the Way to Language* (no. 241), and "The Origin of the Work of Art" (no. 228).

Secondary Sources

349. Deely, John N. *The Tradition Via Heidegger: An Essay on the Meaning of Being in the Philosophy of Martin Heidegger.* The Hague: Martinus Nijhoff, 1971.

350. Feick, Hildegard. *Index zu Heideggers "Sein und Zeit."* Tübingen: Max Niemeyer Verlag, 1972.

351. Gelven, Michael. *Commentary on Heidegger's Being and Time.* New York: Harper & Row, Harper Torchbooks, 1970.

352. Macomber, W. B. *Anatomy of Disillusion: Martin Heidegger's Notion of Truth.* Evanston, Ill.: Northwestern Univ. Pr., 1967.

353. Magnus, Bernd. *Heidegger's Metahistory of Philosophy: Amor Fati, Being and Truth.* The Hague: Martinus Nijhoff, 1970.

354. Marx, Werner. *Heidegger and the Tradition.* Translated by Theodore Kisiel and Murray Greene. Evanston, Ill.: Northwestern Univ. Pr., 1971.

355. Versenyi, Laszlo. *Heidegger, Being, and Truth.* New Haven: Yale Univ. Pr., 1965.

356. Vycinas, Vincent. *Earth and Gods: An Introduction to the Philosophy of Martin Heidegger.* The Hague: Martinus Nijhoff, 1969.

See the complete bibliography in William J. Richardson, *Heidegger: Through Phenomenology to Thought* (no. 91); *also see* nos. 72, 73, 85, 92, 118, 154.

KARL JASPERS
Primary Sources

357. *Existentialism and Humanism.* Translated by E. B. Ashton. New York: Moore, 1952.

358. *The Future of Mankind.* Translated by E. B. Ashton. Chicago: Univ. of Chicago Pr., 1961.

359. *The Great Philosophers.* Translated by Ralph Manheim. New York: Harcourt, Brace, 1962.

360. *The Idea of the University.* Translated by H. A. T. Reiche and H. F. Vanderschmidt. Boston: Beacon, 1959.

361. *Man in the Modern Age.* Translated by Eden and Cedar Paul. London: Routledge & Kegan Paul, 1959.

362. *The Origin and Goal of History.* Translated by Michael Bullock. New Haven: Yale Univ. Pr., 1959.

363. *The Perennial Scope of Philosophy.* Translated by Ralph Manheim. London: Routledge & Kegan Paul, 1950.

364. *Philosophical Faith and Revelation.* Translated by E. B. Ashton. London: Collins, 1967.

365. *Philosophy.* 3 vols. Translated by E. B. Ashton. Chicago: Univ. of Chicago Pr., 1969–71.

366. *Philosophy Is for Every Man.* Translated by R. F. C. Hull and G. Wels. London: Hutchinson, 1969.

367. *Philosophy of Existence.* Translated by Richard F. Grabau. Philadelphia: Univ. of Pennsylvania Pr., 1971.

368. *Reason and Anti-Reason in Our Time.* Translated by Stanley Godman. New Haven: Yale Univ. Pr., 1952.

369. *Reason and Existenz.* Translated by William Earle. New York: Noonday, 1955.

370. *Truth and Symbol.* Translated by Jean T. Wilde et al. New Haven: New Haven College & Univ. Pr., 1959.

371. *Way to Wisdom.* Translated by Ralph Manheim. New Haven: Yale Univ. Pr., 1951.

Secondary Sources

372. Long, Eugene T. *Jaspers and Bultmann: A Dialogue between Philosophy and Theology in the Existentialist Tradition.* Durham, N.C.: Duke Univ. Pr., 1968.

373. Samay, Sebastian. *Reason Revisited: The Philosophy of Karl Jaspers.* Notre Dame, Ind: Univ. of Notre Dame Pr., 1971.

374. Schilpp, Paul Arthur, ed. *Karl Jaspers.* New York: Tudor, 1957.

375. Schrag, Oswald O. *Existence, Existenz, and Transcendence: An Introduction to the Philosophy of Karl Jaspers.* Pittsburgh: Duquesne Univ. Pr., 1971.

GABRIEL MARCEL
Primary Sources

376. *Being and Having.* Translated by Katharine Farrer. Boston: Beacon, 1951.

377. *The Decline of Wisdom.* Translated by Manya Harari. London: Harvill Pr., 1954.

378. *Existential Background of Human Dignity.* Cambridge, Mass.: Harvard Univ. Pr., 1963.

379. *Homo Viator.* Translated by Emma Crawford. New York: Harper & Row, Harper Torchbooks, 1962.

380. *Man against Mass Society.* Translated by G. S. Fraser. Chicago: Regnery, 1962.

381. *Metaphysical Journal.* Translated by Bernard Wall. Chicago: Regnery, 1952.

382. *Philosophical Fragments 1909–1914 and The Philosopher and Peace.* Translated by Lionel A. Blair. Notre Dame, Ind.: Univ. of Notre Dame Pr., 1965.

383. *The Philosophy of Existence.* Translated by Manya Harari. New York: Philosophical Library, 1949.

384. *The Philosophy of Existentialism.* Translated by Manya Harari. New York: Citadel, 1966.

385. *Presence and Immortality.* Translated by Michael A. Machado. Pittsburgh: Duquesne Univ. Pr., 1967.

386. *Problematic Man.* Translated by Brian Thompson. New York: Herder & Herder, 1967.

387. *Searchings.* New York: Newman, 1967.

Also see *The Mystery of Being,* 2 vols. (no. 253).

Secondary Sources

388. Cain, Seymour. *Gabriel Marcel.* New York: Hillary, 1963.

389. Gallagher, Kenneth T. *The Philosophy of Gabriel Marcel.* New York: Fordham Univ. Pr., 1962.

390. Gilson, Etienne, et al. *Existentialisme Chrétienne: Gabriel Marcel.* Paris: Plon, 1947.

391. Keen, Sam. *Gabriel Marcel.* Richmond, Va.: John Knox, 1967.

392. Lapointe, Francois H. "Bibliography of Gabriel Marcel." *Modern Scholasticism* 49 (1971):23–49.

393. O'Malley, John B. *The Fellowship of Being: An Essay on the Concept of Person in the Philosophy of Gabriel Marcel.* The Hague: Martinus Nijhoff, 1966.

MAURICE MERLEAU-PONTY
Primary Sources

394. *Adventures of the Dialectic.* Translated by Joseph Bien. Evanston, Ill.: Northwestern Univ. Pr., 1973.

395. *In Praise of Philosophy.* Translated by John Wild and James Edie. Evanston, Ill.: Northwestern Univ. Pr., 1963.

396. *Sense and Non-Sense.* Translated by Hubert L. Dreyfus and Patricia Allen Dreyfus. Evanston, Ill.: Northwestern Univ. Pr., 1964.

   Also see *Humanism and Terror* (no. 296), *The Phenomenology of Perception* (nos. 6 and 213), *The Primacy of Perception* (no. 214), *The Prose of the World* (no. 215), *Signs* (no. 234), *The Structure of Behavior* (no. 210), and *The Visible and the Invisible* (no. 216).

Secondary Sources

397. Bannan, John F. *The Philosophy of Merleau-Ponty.* New York: Harcourt, Brace, 1967.

398. Kwant, Remy. *From Phenomenology to Metaphysics.* Pittsburgh: Duquesne Univ. Pr., 1966.

399. ———. *The Phenomenological Philosophy of Merleau-Ponty.* Pittsburgh: Duquesne Univ. Pr., 1963.

400. Lanigan, Richard L. "Maurice Merleau-Ponty Bibliography." *Man and World* 3 (1970):289–319.

401. Lapointe, Francois H. "A Bibliography of Maurice Merleau-Ponty." *Human Inquiries* 11 (1971):63–78.

402. Rabil, Albert, Jr. *Merleau-Ponty: Existentialist of the Social World.* New York: Columbia Univ. Pr., 1967.

   Also see nos. 208, 217, 233.

PAUL RICOEUR
Primary Sources

403. *Le conflit des interprétations: Essais d'herméneutique.* Paris: Editions du Seuil, 1969.

404. *Gabriel Marcel et Karl Jaspers: Philosophie du mystère et philosophie du paradoxe.* Paris: Editions de Temps Présent, 1947.

405. Appendix to *Histoire de la philosophie allemande,* by E. Bréhier. 3d ed. Paris: J. Vrin, 1954.

406. *History and Truth.* Translated by Charles A. Kelbley. Evanston, Ill.: Northwestern Univ. Pr., 1965.

407. With Mikel Dufrenne. *Karl Jaspers et la philosophie de l'existence.* Paris: Editions du Seuil, 1947.

408. With Alasdair MacIntyre. *The Religious Significance of Atheism.* New York: Columbia Univ. Pr., 1969.

   Also see *Freedom and Nature* (no. 203), which is a translation of vol. 1 of *Philosophie de la volonté; Fallible Man* (no. 301), a translation of pt. 1, vol. 2 of *Philosophie de la volonté; The Symbolism of Evil* (no. 290), pt. 2, vol. 2 of *Philosophie de la volonté;* "Sur·la phénoménologie" (no. 7); *Husserl: An Examination of His Philosophy* (no. 52); and *Freud and Philosophy* (no. 269).

Secondary Sources

409. Ihde, Don. *Hermeneutic Phenomenology: The Philosophy of Paul Ricoeur.* Evanston, Ill.: Northwestern Univ. Pr., 1971.

410. Lapointe, Francois H. "A Bibliography on Paul Ricoeur." *Philosophy Today* 17 (1973):176–82.
 Bibliography of articles, reviews, and books on the work of Ricoeur.

411. Rasmussen, David M. *Mythic-Symbolic Language and Philosophical Anthropology: A Constructive Interpretation of the Thought of Paul Ricoeur.* The Hague: Martinus Nijhoff, 1971.

412. Vansina, Dirk F. "Bibliographie de Paul Ricoeur." *Revue philosophique de Louvain* 60 (1962):394–413; 66 (1968):85–101.
 Exhaustive bibliography of Ricoeur's writings in all languages, complete through June 1962.

JEAN-PAUL SARTRE
Primary Sources

413. *Critique de la raison dialectique.* Paris: Gallimard, 1960.

414. *The Emotions: Outline of a Theory.* Translated by Bernard Frechtman. New York: Philosophical Library, 1948.

415. *Literary and Philosophical Essays.* Translated by Annette Michelson. New York: Collier, 1962.

416. *The Philosophy of Existentialism.* Edited by Wade Baskin. New York: Philosophical Library, 1965.

417. *Psychology of the Imagination.* Translated by Bernard Frechtman. New York: Philosophical Library, 1946.

418. *Search for a Method.* Translated by Hazel E. Barnes. New York: Knopf, 1963.

419. *Situations.* New York: Braziller, 1964.

420. *The Words: An Autobiography.* Translated by Bernard Frechtman. Greenwich, Conn.: Fawcett, 1966.

 Also see "Intentionality: A Fundamental Idea of Husserl's Phenomenology" (no. 53), *Being and Nothingness* (no. 199), *The Transcendence of the Ego* (no. 200), *Existentialism* (no. 204), *Literature and Existentialism* (no. 235), and *What Is Literature?* (no. 236). For bibliography of Sartre, *see* nos. 158, 163, and 421.

Secondary Sources

421. Belkind, Allen J. *Jean-Paul Sartre in English: A Bibliographical Guide.* Kent, Ohio: Kent State Univ. Pr., 1970.

422. Cranston, Maurice. *The Quintessence of Sartrism.* New York: Harper & Row, Harper Torchbooks, 1971.

423. Desan, Wilfrid. *The Tragic Finale: An Essay on the Philosophy of Sartre.* Cambridge: Harvard Univ. Pr., 1954.

424. Natanson, Maurice. *A Critique of Jean-Paul Sartre's Ontology.* Lincoln, Neb.: Univ. of Nebraska Pr., 1951.

425. Sheridan, James F. *Sartre: The Radical Conversion.* Athens, Ohio: Ohio Univ. Pr., 1969.

426. Thody, Philip. *Sartre: A Biographical Introduction.* New York: Scribner, 1971.

For additional discussion of Sartre's philosophy, *see* the bibliography in chapter 4; for Sartre's esthetics, *see* no. 233.

SUPPLEMENT
TO THE SECOND
EDITION

Of the making of books there is no end, said the preacher. And that was before the days of word processors, desktop publishing, and high speed offset printing. In the fifteen or so years since *Exploring Phenomenology* was published, the literature dealing with phenomenology has continued to grow, and there is now a need to update the bibliographical offerings of the original volume to take account of the expanding body of literature dealing with phenomenology and phenomenological themes.

Like its first edition, this second edition of *Exploring Phenomenology* makes no claim to comprehensiveness. What we offer here is a selection of the fifty or so works that we think give the best indication of the continued work in phenomenology since the early 70s. If we have left out important works, all we can say is that this is a guide, not a comprehensive listing. It is a guide designed for acquisition librarians and for students interested in the latest writings on phenomenological philosophy. It centers on books, not on journal articles. The latter can be researched in one of several biographical tools that have been either added or greatly expanded since the first edition of this book. *The Philosophers Index,* for example, has not only been extended backwards in time to the 1940s but is also available on a computer data base.

A second edition of this book also calls for reflection on the "phenomenological movement" itself. The quotations around this phrase not only are intended to give credit to such pioneering writers as Herbert Spiegelberg, who uses it in his history of phenomenology, but also to indicate that we are less sanguine about referring to phenomenological philosophy as a movement than we were fifteen years ago. That is not to say that phenomenology is any less prevalent in American universities. If anything, it is more so. But what has changed in the last fifteen years is the attitude toward method. Today philosophers seem more open to looking at a philosophical work regardless of the methodological approaches of its author and judging it on the basis of its outcome. Many philosophers, especially the younger members of the profession, are less interested in labeling themselves phenomenologists, analytic philosophers, ordinary language philosophers, or whatever. Philosophical interest seems to be shifting toward the desire to deal with philosophical problems, less on inspecting the relative merits of the methodology of the philosopher. This is not universally true, however, and fierce quarrels can still break out between proponents of philosophical methodologies that are seen as rivals. Yet there seems to be a developing spirit of openness among philosophers to alternative ways of doing philosophy.[1]

---

1. In this regard, see Richard Rorty, "Philosophy in America Today," in *Consequences of Pragmatism* (Minneapolis: University of Minnesota Press, 1982), pp. 211–30.

One thing that is clearer now than it was fifteen years ago is that existentialism, as philosophy, reflecting what the Germans call the *Zeitgeist* of the middle part of this century, gave expression to a set of concerns that no longer seem dominant in contemporary philosophical thought. There is additional literature dealing with important existential philosophers, and representative titles from this body of literature have been included in the bibliographical entries. But it is safe to say that few contemporary philosophers would characterize themselves as existentialists any more than contemporary philosophers would willingly accept the designation positivist.[2] The books dealing with existential philosophy now have a historical orientation to them that places them generally in the background of discussion of contemporary issues. Part of the reason for this is the death of the principal existentialist figures: Sartre, Marcel, Heidegger, just to name three, since the first edition of this book appeared.

Much of the literature we include in the updated bibliographical entries is what we could call mainstream phenomenology, that is, works dealing with the issues raised by the first generation of phenomenologists and those who extended phenomenological methods to other philosophical issues. Two currents that were present in phenomenology fifteen years ago but have now become much more dominant in the literature are hermeneutics, as a way of doing philosophy, and the relation between philosophy and the social sciences. Both of these themes have phenomenological roots and are providing new ways for philosophy to speak to a wider set of concerns.

Because phenomenological philosophy so dominated the intellectual climate of Europe in the years since World War II, it is an easy error to see all philosophical trends in Europe as having phenomenological roots and therefore as being extensions of phenomenology. This is a danger that is not easily overcome, especially since many of the thinkers of such movements as postmodernism and deconstructionism received much of their initial inspiration from phenomenological philosophy. Further compounding the difficulty is that such contemporary philosophers as Jacques Derrida wrote on phenomenological themes earlier in their career. These thinkers are also often lumped together with more traditional phenomenologists under the general rubric "continental philosophy." But to label such offshoots phenomenological is to blur the distinctions between phenomenology and nonphenomenological approaches in such a way as to be confusing at best and erroneous at worst. Such recent or contemporary French thinkers as Foucault and Derrida are doing something very different than phenomenological philosophy, even though it is possible to trace their philosophical underpinnings to Husserl and Heidegger.[3]

2. See Paul Edward's claim in *The Encyclopedia of Philosophy* that logical positivism is dead, "or as dead as a philosophical movement ever becomes." Vol. 5, entry under the heading "Logical Positivism."

3. In this regard, see the excellent work by Hubert L. Dreyfus and Paul Rabinow, *Michel Foucault: Beyond Structuralism and Hermeneutics* (Chicago: The University of Chicago Press, 1982), especially pp. 50–51.

Occasionally they will use such phenomenological phrases as "bracketing," but beyond such verbal parallels, there is little in their work that could be consciously labeled as phenomenological.

In contrast to the hermeneutics of a philosopher such as Paul Ricoeur, the text interpretation offered by the deconstructionist movement destroys the possibility of any single meaning to the text. The text itself must be deconstructed, taken apart, so that the components of it can be seen as part of that larger universe of signs. The text, which has no privileged meaning, must disappear into the vast network of signs. There is no importance to be given to the author of the text or to the interests of the reader of the text, and there is no privileged meaning to a text, any text. That this is an appealing ploy in literary criticism is obvious, since the entire literary corpus is available for restudy and deconstruction, thereby providing fertile soil to be plowed by an entire new generation of scholars. It is important to note, however, that deconstructionism is much more popular, and influential, in the United States than it is in Europe. And in those American universities where deconstruction is a practiced form of criticism, the practitioners tend to be in the departments of literature, not departments of philosophy.

HERMENEUTICS

A theme present in phenomenological philosophy fifteen years ago that has emerged with considerable force as an application of phenomenological approaches is that of hermeneutics as a way of doing philosophy. The first edition of this book made passing mention of hermeneutics (see p. 145), but now the literature in this growing area demands more extensive treatment.

The term hermeneutics is almost as old as Western philosophy itself, going back to Aristotle's treatise *On Interpretation,* known to us usually by its Latin title *De Interpretatione,* which is only a Latinization of the original Greek title *Peri Hermeneias.* As used by Aristotle, hermeneutics pertained to the rules and principles for interpreting texts. The word itself derives from the Greek god Hermes, the messenger who interpreted the messages of the gods to humanity. As Richard Palmer points out, "The various forms of the word suggest the process of bringing a thing or situation from unintelligibility to understanding. The Greeks credited Hermes with the discovery of language and writing—the tools which human understanding employs to grasp meaning and to convey it to others." [4] Apart from Aristotle's use of the term, hermeneutics found its main application to be the task of interpreting religious texts.

Hermeneutics remained largely a discipline of interpreting sacred texts until well into the nineteenth century. It was then that the notion of hermeneutics was expanded by the German philosopher Wilhelm Dilthey to include as its

4. Richard Palmer, *Hermeneutics* (Evanston: Northwestern University Press, 1969), p. 13.

proper object of inquiry realities other than written texts. Dilthey suggested that the approach to a study of culture should be a hermeneutic one. The artifacts of a culture—its monuments, inscriptions, documents, and so forth—provide material for historians, but the question Dilthey raised was how one should deal with such materials. One way would be to fashion historical inquiry after the model of the natural sciences, that is, looking for the laws that provide a basis for a science of historical interpretation in a way that is analogous to the natural scientist's search for the eternal laws of nature. Dilthey saw clearly, however, that historical science would have to be based on a different foundation than the natural sciences inasmuch as it dealt with cultural life, that is, the way individual human beings respond in different ways to the particular historical epoch in which they find themselves. Dilthey introduced the distinction between explanation (*Erklaren*) and understanding (*Verstehen*), the former referring to the domain of the natural sciences with their empirical methods and inductive logic, the latter relating to the realm of the spiritual.

A further enlargement of hermeneutics as a way of dealing with philosophical themes was offered by Martin Heidegger, who suggested that all human activity provides a field for interpretation. But what is to be interpreted is not just human activity but the possibilities of being. Like much of Heidegger, this thought is somewhat obscure, but to understand his expanded notion of hermeneutics, imagine a circle that represents a written, perhaps sacred, text. This circle is contained within a larger circle which represents all the artifacts of a culture. Finally both are included within a larger circle which is human existence itself, an interpretation of which opens up an understanding of one's possibilities of being.

A hermeneutical approach—whether to a text or a culture—shows its phenomenological roots by the refusal to bring to the task of interpretation a set of assumptions about the text itself. The text addresses us from a different time, sometimes in a different language or from a different culture, but we read it with the expectation that we can bridge these gaps. Yet the task of interpretation is not one of trying to reconstruct the world of the text but to let the text speak to the interests of the reader. Again we can see the echoes of phenomenological approaches; it is neither possible nor desirable to treat the text as an objective datum and the reader as an independent subject. The task of interpretation involves a dialectical process that includes the interests of the reader as well as the autonomy of the text. To sacrifice either pole of this continuum is to fail to understand the text.

A philosopher whose work on hermeneutics has greatly expanded in the last fifteen years is Paul Ricoeur, whose works are listed in the section on hermeneutics. Ricoeur began his work on interpretation theory by dealing with literature infused with symbolic elements, first the language of religion, then the language of dream interpretation as practiced by psychoanalysis. His later work has centered on the ways new meanings emerge in language through the metaphorical process and on the role of time in the narrative structure of texts.

Philosophical Hermeneutics

The expansion of hermeneutics from written texts to other human constructions has given rise to two hermeneutical schools. The one, known as *philosophical hermeneutics,* is followed by those who consider themselves purists. The second school, known as *methodological hermeneutics,* is a more historically oriented approach. The differences between the two trends in hermeneutics cannot be given a final reading since thinkers in these two areas are still engaged in critical writing and are continuously modifying their positions. But it is possible to characterize each broadly and with reference to their general points of departure.

Philosophical hermeneutics reflects the influence of Heidegger and is led by such thinkers as Hans Georg Gadamer, Otto Poeggeler, Karl Heinz Volkmann-Schluck and partially by Ernst Wolfgang Orth, Karl-Otto Apel, Hugh J. Silverman, Thomas Sheehan, and John Sallis. Basic to philosophical hermeneutics is the attempt to discover and explicate the prejudgments that are inherent in various philosophical systems and the languages in which they are expressed. These prejudgments constitute our own historical horizons and comprise a preunderstanding that is taken for granted in all that humans do and think. It is not possible to extricate ourselves from such prejudgments since neither thought nor action is possible without them. Such a view amounts to a severe critique of phenomenology, which had attempted initially to be free from presuppositions.

Consider, for example, any particular science. Its understanding of its own activity is tied up with such prejudgments as the view that there is a given, an objective factor that can be described and articulated in terms of its essence. But philosophical hermeneutics would argue that even the term "essence" is an interpretation and reflects a particular historical horizon involving more meaning than any one individual could encompass. Phenomenology cannot make a claim of offering a complete and exhaustive account of all awareness. Among other reasons, this is not possible due to the difficulty of extricating oneself from a particular tradition. Mohanty has pointed out the difficulty that philosophical hermeneutics even has of making this claim, for to say that "it is impossible to extricate oneself from one's own historical tradition" is to make an "essential" claim.

Philosophical hermeneutics has other problems as well. It is difficult to interpret the texts of the past without abandoning the claim that one is bound to one's historical tradition. This is to say that any text would have to be interpreted in terms of our current historical context. But even if we claim to have understood a given text, this would mean that we are interpreting the text by producing another text, leading to a continuous production of texts that do not tell us anything about the texts that are being analyzed. In principle one must claim either that the new text is a repetition of the preunderstanding of a given tradition, or that there is simply the proliferation of different texts, none of which has any inherent link to the others since all are creations reflecting the historical horizon of the interpreter.

Some have readily embraced this latter alternative, leading to the procedure called deconstruction. Already referred to in the preceding discussion, deconstruction amounts to a total rejection of the view that a text has an essential meaning that can be translated and extricated from its linguistic, historical, and cultural context. The basic claim is that since all thought is linguistic, there are no languages that would signify anything; all language is simply a play of metaphors upon metaphors, and a text is to be seen as a part of the larger universe of signs. Even metaphors are not recognizable as such, since to be a metaphor requires a univocal meaning which the metaphor destroys. As has already been mentioned, deconstruction cannot be classified as a type of phenomenology even though some of its proponents may claim phenomenological roots.

Methodological Hermeneutics

Whereas philosophical hermeneutics claims it is not a method that can be applied to other disciplines, methodological hermeneutics gives primacy to methodological procedures in order to achieve an accurate reading of historical "texts." As has already been mentioned, the term "text" here refers to more than a linguistic document. Scientific works, social systems, aesthetic creations, mythological morphologies, and so forth are objectifications of human activity. As such, these objectification are accessible to interpretations provided that strict rules are applied. The first rule is to exclude one's own historical and situational context as the means of interpretation. The second rule is commonly referred to as "reading the text within its own context." The meaning of any specific term or factor makes sense and can be grasped if the context of the text is equally considered.

Methodological hermeneutics not only offers a more fruitful alternative to philosophical hermeneutics, it also is a corrective to Husserlian phenomenology. We may recall Husserl's efforts to deal with the "other," other human beings, beginning first with the fact of the other's embodiment and then as a bearer of psychological states, mental capacities, and finally cultural traits. The difficulties Husserl confronted were due to the priority of the physical over the expressive. Methodological hermeneutics gives priority to *meanings*. That is, any access to the other is not principally bodily or perceptual but through the significative and the cultural-intersubjective.

Some phenomenologists, such as Ludwig Landgrebe, have acquired a standing as creators of their own school. His school has tackled such issues as the constitution of history and issues of theology. Another major thinker who has not, however, appeared in English translation is Eugen Fink. His work is difficult and somewhat directed away from issues considered in the mainstream of phenomenological development. His unique contribution has been to question the fundamental ontological direction of the Western tradition. The ontological concerns of the tradition, that is, concern for Being, and beings (in Heidegger's sense) left little room for such cosmic phenomena as space, time, and movement. These cosmic phenomena are not expressible in ontologically oriented terms and cannot even be regarded as "phenomena." Nonetheless, Fink unfolds an entirely unique phenomenological hermeneutics of such basic issues, and it is hoped that his work will eventually receive wider attention.

PHILOSOPHY AND
THE SOCIAL SCIENCES

Perhaps one of the most active areas of phenomenological activity during the past fifteen years has been in the social sciences. The connection between hermeneutics and a philosophy of the social sciences as Dilthey originally used the term has already been mentioned. To understand the term almost literally, we would say that we "read" a culture from its artifacts; we do speak of "reading someone like a book," or of understanding what people are up to by interpreting their movements and gestures. This is a crude explanation of a hermeneutic approach to the social sciences. Again, as in the case of text interpretation, the proper approach to a culture is not to come to a study of it with a set of methodological assumptions or expect to view it in an entirely objective way.

The social sciences, and above all communications, have moved away from concern with "pure" questions of consciousness to the more ambiguous domains of bodily, expressive interaction. Such a move has been a welcome reprieve from the all-too-abstract "conditions for the possibility" (transcendental phenomenology) and "light of being" (eidetic phenomenology) toward the sort of activities that are directly lived and interconnected. This is not to say that phenomenology has lost sight of theoretical issues but rather that theoretical issues are situated in their concrete contexts. For example, some proponents of hermeneutics charged that phenomenology had become too abstract and concerned itself only with linguistic subtleties and distinctions. The turn toward activity, pragmatic engagement and praxis is premised on the notion that the "I can" is more fundamental than the "I think." The reasons for this claim are many, but first among them is a change in the notion of "fact." No longer is fact to be considered as a brute datum but rather as an interconnected system of meanings. This leads to the recognition that the human body is not just a sum of mechanical facts but an active process of conscious organization within the field of meaningful phenomena.

A second change occurs in the notion of the ego. Existential phenomenologists, such as Sartre, followed Husserl's description of the ego to a conclusion that led to the self as a nothingness, an absence. But quite apart from these logistic arguments is the recognition of a more fundamental experience of the self as belonging to *my experience*. This body is *my* body, these feelings are *my* feelings, this image in the mirror is *me*. Even before reflection on one's ego, one is already acquiring abilities on the basis of movements, explorations, probing and testing, reaching, and correcting the movements in tasks that are interactive processes. In short, individuation is not premised on the givenness of a brute, factual, mechanical body or associated in some mysterious way to the self. Rather individuation proceeds from conscious bodily activities that function in a system of tasks and meaningful orientations.

A third element in the shift from the pure to the applied is found in the concept of action itself. Phenomenology offers functional, not merely physical, models for activities. An active being resists the division of self into consciousness and body, ego and its possessions, self and its characteristics. All these distinctions are translated into dynamic activities where every conscious project is equally a call for the corporeal "I can." Embodied consciousness is seen as the necessary point of departure for any analysis of the world of lived experience, specifically the practical world.

These conceptual shifts within phenomenology prepare the way for phenomenological methods to be applied to such fields as communication and pedagogy. Both of these fields place great emphasis on intersubjectivity and extend into such fields as language, culture, traditions of values, and political systems. Using insights from both Husserl and Merleau-Ponty, phenomenologists in these fields have expended the diadic model of communication into a triadic model; one speaks to another human being (diadic) but with an intention, speaking about *something*. In teaching there is the teacher, the one taught, and that which is taught, the subject matter. In this sense the dialogical interaction of sender-receiver of messages had to be supplemented by the introduction of intentional awareness of the meant world.

BIBLIOGRAPHICAL SUPPLEMENT

Since the chapter topics of the first edition have seemed to function well as organizational principles for the bibliographical entries, we will continue to follow the broad outlines of the first edition. This will allow students or librarians to update the areas in which they are most interested.

General Themes of Phenomenology

S1. Apel, Karl-Otto. *Towards a Transformation of Philosophy,* translated by Glyn Adey and David Frisby. London: Routledge & Kegan Paul, 1980.

Discusses the transformation of transcendental phenomenology by hermeneutics, the embracing of hermeneutics of linguistics, and the transcendental necessity of communication for interpreting society.

S2. Funke, Gerhard. *Phenomenology: Metaphysics or Method?* Translated by J. David Parent. Athens: Ohio Univ. Pr., 1987.
Discusses the conflict between those who see phenomenology primarily as a method and those who see it is a science with its own independent subject matter.

S3. Hiroshi, Kojima, editor. *Phaenomenologie der Praxis im Dialog Zuiwshen Japan und dem Westen.* Wuerzburg: Koenigschausen & Neumann, 1989.
Contains writings in English and German on practical phenomenology by philosophers from Japan, Europe, and the United States.

S4. Ihde, Don and Richard Zaner, editors. *Dialogues in Phenomenology.* The Hague: Nijhoff, 1975.
Collection of essays by analytical and phenomenological philosophers exploring issues common to both traditions.

S5. Landgrebe, Ludwig. *Faktizitaet und Individuation: Studien zu den Grundlagen der Phaenomenologie.* Hamburg: Felix Meiner Verlag, 1982.
Critical reflections on the essence on history and specifically on the problem of individuation and intersubjectivity.

S6. Mohanty, J.N., *The Possibility of Transcendental Philosophy.* Dordrecht: Martinus Nijhoff, 1985.
Discusses various trends in American and continental philosophies and refutes challenges from neopositivists who claim that transcendental philosophy is impossible.

S7. Pičvević, Edo, editor. *Phenomenology and philosophical Understanding.* New York: Cambridge: Cambridge Univ. Pr., 1975.
Collection of articles by philosophers from both the analytic and phenomenological traditions showing both the similarities and differences in the two approaches to philosophy.

S8. Spiegelberg, Herbert. *The Context of the Phenomenological Movement.* The Hague: Martinus Nijhoff, 1981.
Discusses the historical and philosophical backgrounds of phenomenology.

S9. Waldenfels, Bernhard, M. Jan Brockman, and Ante Pazanin, editors. *Phenomenology and Marxism.* Translated by Claude J. Evans. London: Routledge & Kegan Paul, 1984.
Selections from a four-volume work in German dealing with the contemporary encounter between phenomenology and marxism.

*Husserl and the
Phenomenological Movement*

S10. Cairns, Dorian. *Conversations with Husserl and Fink.* Edited by the Husserl Archives in Louvain. Foreword by Richard M. Zaner. The Hague: Martinus Nijhoff, 1976.

Important records of the thoughts of one of Husserl's earliest disciples.

S11. de Boer, Theodore. *The Development of Husserl's Thought.* Translated by T. Plantinga. The Hague: Martinus Nijhoff, 1978.

Good discussion of the full range of Husserl's work.

S12. Edie, James M. *Edmund Husserl's Phenomenology.* Bloomington: Indiana Univ. Pr., 1987.

Written in accessible language, this book offers a sympathetic although critical overview of the major work of Husserl.

S13. Elliston, Frederick A. and Peter McCormick, editors. *Husserl: Expositions and Appraisals.* Notre Dame: Univ. of Notre Dame Pr., 1977.

Collection of essays on Husserl's thought written by noted Husserl scholars who reflect all the traditions of interpreting Husserl.

S14. Kohák, Erazim Vaclav. *Idea and Experience: Edmund Husserl's Project of Phenomenology in Ideas I.* Chicago: Univ. of Chicago Pr., 1978.

Good introduction to Husserl's thought as expressed in his major work *Ideas.*

S15. McKenna, William R. *Husserl's Introductions to Phenomenology: Interpretation and Critique.* The Hague: Martinus Nijhoff, 1982.

General discussion of Husserl's phenomenological method.

S16. Mohanty, J. N., editor. *Readings on E. Husserl's Logical Investigations.* The Hague: Martinus Nijhoff, 1977.

Collection of essays by Husserlian scholars on the difficult issues raised in Husserl's discussion of logic.

S17. Natanson, Maurice. *Edmund Husserl: Philosopher of Infinite Tasks.* Evanston: Northwestern Univ. Pr., 1973.

Winner of a National Book Award, this work is an excellent introduction to the thought of Husserl for those unfamiliar with his work.

S18. Stroker, Elisabeth von, editor. *Husserlian Foundations of Science.* Translated by Hardy Lee. Washington: Univ. Pr. of America, 1987.

Analysis and extension of Husserl's phenomenological approach to science to include psychology, the natural sciences, and history.

Hermeneutics

S19. Bleicher, Joseph. *Contemporary Hermeneutics.* London: Routledge & Kegan Paul, 1980.

A critical updating of the development of hermeneutics; contains excellent bibliography.

S20. Caputo, John D. *Radical Hermeneutics: Repetition, Deconstruction, and the Hermeneutic Project*. Bloomington: Indiana Univ. Pr., 1987.
Shows how some interpreters of phenomenology have made a turn away from hermeneutics toward the dissolution of philosophy and the appearance of post-metaphysical thinking.

S21. Ihde, Don. *Techniques and Praxis*. Boston: D. Reidel, 1979.
Develops phenomenological hermeneutics from the side of practical application and even experimentation and shows that phenomenological research need not shun scientific and technical questions.

S22. Ricoeur, Paul. *Essays on Biblical Interpretation*. Edited by Lewis S. Mudge. Philadelphia: Fortress Pr., 1980.
Collection of four essays by Ricoeur on the hermeneutics of biblical texts.

S23. Ricoeur, Paul. *Time and Narrative*. Translated by Kathleen McLaughlin and David Pellauer. Chicago: The Univ. of Chicago Pr., vol. 1, 1984; vol. 2, 1985; vol. 3, 1988.
Study of time and narrative in historical writing and fiction; spans the philosophical study of literary form from Aristotle to Heidegger.

S24. Ricoeur, Paul. Du texte à l'action: Essais d'hermeneutique, II. Paris: Seuil, 1986.
A collection of articles by Ricoeur dealing with a wide range of issues in hermeneutics; continues the collection started by No. 403.

S25. Thompson, John B. *Critical Hermeneutics: A Study in the Thought of Paul Ricoeur and Jurgen Habermas*. Cambridge: Cambridge Univ. Pr., 1981.
Comparative study of Wittgenstein, Ricoeur, and Habermas.

S26. Weinsheimer, Joel C. *Gadamer's Hermeneutics*. New Haven: Yale Univ. Pr., 1985.
Clear and careful exposition of Gadamer's major work *Truth and Method* showing the importance of historical understanding at various levels.

Phenomenology and the Social Sciences

S27. Bien, Joseph. *Phenomenology and the Social Sciences: A Dialogue*. The Hague: Martinus Nijhoff, 1978.
Collection of essays showing how phenomenology has affected the social sciences, especially in Europe.

S28. Boehler, Dietrich. *Rekonstruktive Pragmatik: Von der Bewusstseins Philosophie sur Communikationsreflexion*. Frankfurt: Suhrkamp, 1985)

Incorporates such concerns as dialogue and norms for understanding human interaction.

S29. Fink, Eugen. *Erziehungswissenschaft und Lebenslehre*. Freiburg: Verlag Rombach, 1970.

Ties pedagogy to various ontologies, social systems, even mythic concepts, while offering foundations for education by challenging the claims of pedagogy to be a science.

S30. Fink, Eugen. *Grundfragen der Systematischen Paedagogik*. Freiburg: Verlag Rombach, 1978.

Evaluates various ontological psychological, and mythological theses on education.

S31. Fink, Eugen. *Grundphaenomene des Menschlichen Daseins*. Freiburg: Verlag Karl Alber, 1979.

Offers Fink's fundamental philosophical anthropology dealing with the self and others, time and death, society and labor, play and domination, eros and self-understanding.

S32. Grathoff, Richard and Bernhard Waldenfels, editors. *Soziulituet und Intersub-jectivitaet*. Munich: Wilhelm Fink Verlag, 1983.

Contributions on social phenomenology by scholars from various nations and disciplines.

S33. Ricoeur, Paul. *Hermeneutics and the Social Sciences*. Edited and translated by John B. Thompson. Cambridge: Cambridge Univ. Pr., 1981.

A new translation of Ricoeur's articles that apply principles of hermeneutics to human action and its social contexts.

S34. Ricoeur, Paul. *Lectures on Ideology and Utopia*. Edited by George H. Taylor. New York: Columbia Univ. Pr., 1986.

Critique of Marx, Mannheim, Saint-Simon and Fourier with extended discussions of Althusser, Weber, Habermas, and Geertz.

Phenomenology Applied
to Other Disciplines

S35. Dufrenne, Mikel. *In the Presence of the Sensuous*. Translated by Mark S. Roberts and Dennis Gallagher. Atlantic Highlands: Humanities Pr., 1989.

Includes essays on aesthetics in which the author argues for the irreducibility of human and aesthetic experience and engages in a dialogue with contemporary philosophical movements.

S36. Geiger, Moritz. *The Significance of Art: A Phenomenological Approach to Aesthetics*. Edited and translated by Kalus Berger. Washington: Univ. Pr. of America, 1986.

First English version of Geiger's phenomenology in general and aesthetics in particular; Geiger was one of the main figures in the Munich school of phenomenology.

S37. Ihde, Don and Richard Zaner, editors. *Interdisciplinary Phenomenology.* The Hague: Martinus Nijhoff, 1977.
Essays from different authors showing how phenomenological approaches can be applied to nonphilosophical undertakings.

S38. Ihde, Don. *Experimental Phenomenology.* New York: G.P. Putnams's Sons, Capricorn Books, 1977.
Application of phenomenological methods to a study of vision.

S39. Pilotta, Joseph J. and Algis Mickunas. *Science of Communication: Its Phenomenological Foundation.* Hillsdale: Lawrence Erlbaum, 1990.
Critique of other approaches and application of phenomenological method to the various levels of communication.

S40. Ingarten, Roman. *Ontology of the Work of Art.* Translated by Raymond Meyer with John T. Goldthwait. Athens: Ohio univ. Pr., 1989.
Subtitled "The Musical Work, the Picture, the Architectural Work, the Film," this is a classic study of phenomenological approaches to aesthetic judgment.

S41. Jonas, Hans. *Das Prinzip Verantwortung.* Frankfurt: Insel Verlag, 1984.
Expands the phenomenological tradition of the crises of modern science toward ethical issues in technology and raises important questions concerning the "rights" of nature.

S42. Jones, Edwin. *Reading the Book of Nature: A Phenomenological Study of Creative Expression in Science and Painting.* Athens: Ohio Univ. Pr., 1989.
Uses Heidegger and Husserl to understand creativity in natural science and in art; Galileo and Cezanne are used to illustrate the phenomenological approach.

S43. Lanigan, Richard. *Phenomenology of Communication.* Pittsburgh: Duquesne Univ. Pr., 1988.
Combines Merleau-Ponty's thesis of field, sign, and critique of the objectivist illusion with the contributions of semiotics and structuralism to offer a meta-theory of communications.

S44. Meyer-Drawe, Kaete. *Leiblichkeit und Sozialidtaet.* Munich: Wilhelm Fink Verlag, 1984.
Analyzes the prescientific bases of intersubjectivity and the way it functions in the pedagogical setting and in child development theories.

S45. Ricoeur, Paul. *The Rule of Metaphor: Multi-disciplinary Studies of the Creation of Meaning in Language.* Translated by Robert Czerny with Kathleen McLaughlin and John Costello. Toronto: Univ. of Toronto Pr., 1975.

Historically oriented study challenging the claims of the rhetorical tradition that metaphor is merely ornamental.

S46. Schrag, Calvin O., *Communicative Praxis and the Space of Subjectivity.* Bloomington: Indiana Univ. Pr., 1988.
Expands hermeneutics toward communication theory and practice; an excellent source for the post-modernist and modernist controversy.

S47. Stroeker, Elisabeth. *Investigations in the Philosophy of Space.* Translated by Algis Mickunas. Athens: Ohio Univ. Pr., 1987.
Connects various modes of experience and their correlative spaces in an effort to show that the human is a Euclidean being.

Works on Individual Philosophers

S48. Detmer, David. *Freedom as Value: A Critique of the Ethical Theory of Jean-Paul Sartre.* Peru: Open Court, 1988.
Argues that Sartre was consistent in his conception of freedom throughout his works and that freedom is the highest value.

S49. Hanley, Katharine R., *Dramatic Approaches to Creative Fidelity: A Study in the Theater and Philosophy of Gabriel Marcel.* Washington: Univ. Pr. of America, 1987.
Shows the relationship between Marcel's philosophical and theatrical writings by using the theme of creative fidelity.

S50. Kockelmans, Joseph J. *Heidegger and Science.* Washington: Univ. Pr. of America, 1985.
Focuses on Heidegger's conceptions of the ontological foundations of the natural and social sciences.

S51. Lapointe, Francois and Claire Lapointe, editors. *Jean-Paul Sartre and His Critics: An International Bibliography (1938–1975).* Bowling Green, OH: Philosophy Documentation Center, 1975.
Bibliography of books and articles devoted to Sartre's literary and philosophical writings. Entries are in both English and European languages.

S52. Madison, Gary Brent. *The Phenomenology of Merleau-Ponty.* Athens: Ohio Univ. Pr., 1981.
Published first in French and translated by the author, this work is perhaps the most comprehensive and most readable survey of Merleau-Ponty's work available.

S53. Reagan, Charles, editor. *Studies in the Philosophy of Paul Ricoeur.* Athens: Ohio Univ. Pr., 1981.
Collection of essays by twelve interpreters of Ricoeur's thought.

S54. Vansina, Franz D. *Paul Ricoeur: A Primary and Secondary Systematic Bibliography 1935–1984*. Louvain: Éditions Peeters, 1985.

A comprehensive bibliography of all of Ricoeur's writings in all languages.

S55. Zimmerman, Michael E. *Eclipse of the Self: The Development of Heidegger's Concept of Authenticity*. Athens: Ohio Univ. Pr., 1981.

A highly readable analysis of Heidegger's notion of the self.

INDEX

**A NOTE
ABOUT THE AUTHORS**

Algis Mickunas is professor of philosophy at Ohio University where he teaches courses in phenomenology, philosophy of culture, and contemporary German philosophy. His other books include *Science of Communication: Its Phenomenological Foundation* and translations of several philosophical works by European authors.

David Stewart is professor of philosophy at Ohio University and teaches courses in ethics, religion and contemporary French philosophy. He is co-editor of *The Philosophy of Paul Ricoeur: An Anthology of His Work* and his publications include articles on hermeneutical approaches to religion.